Margaret Scholl

The Bildungsdrama of the Age of Goethe

# German Studies in America

Edited by Heinrich Meyer

No. 21

Margaret Scholl
The Bildungsdrama of the Age of Goethe

Herbert Lang Bern
Peter Lang Frankfurt/M.

# The Bildungsdrama
## of the
## Age of Goethe

by
Margaret Scholl

Herbert Lang Bern
Peter Lang Frankfurt/M.

ISBN 3 261 01857 7

© Herbert Lang & Co. Ltd., Bern (Switzerland)
Peter Lang Ltd., Frankfurt/M. (West-Germany)
1976. All rights reserved.

Printed by Lang Druck Ltd., Liebefeld/Bern (Switzerland)

## DEDICATION

To the Scholls in my life

# PREFACE

During the period of Storm and Stress, as German literature underwent many great changes, the figure of the Young Man, inexperienced in life and headed for a collision with it, was for the first time in the history of the drama put on the stage in significant numbers as dramatic hero. Initially, he was portrayed as a man of unrestrained feeling, but as the period developed and then outgrew itself, the Young Man changed with it. He changed because he was forced to compromise with his social setting, which was often portrayed as an established court. The change in the Young Man took the form of recognizing a validity in established order, and in relinquishing his philosophy of complete personal freedom. Whether the change made him "better" or not can be disputed, but coming to terms with his life now meant coming to an understanding with the common community that held him captive. This process of growth and self- and community-recognition occurred frequently enough in post Storm and Stress drama to justify its identification with the title "Bildungsdrama."

Three plays from the Age of Goethe are selected to document these assertions. Using Schiller's DON CARLOS, Goethe's TORQUATO TASSO, and Kleist's PRINZ FRIEDRICH VON HOMBURG as points of arrival, the literary image of the Young Man is traced as he developed from an unteachable to a teachable figure. The authors' intent to portray this progression is demonstrated through historical and literary references from the authors' own lives and works, and the philosophical and "period" differences between Kleist and Goethe-Schiller are taken into account. The actual mechanics of the "Bildung" in the three individual plays are then defined individually and compared collectively, and it is shown how all three plays contain a like configuration of many factors, above all the court as general antagonist, and the personal antagonist-beloved woman as "teacher" figures. The process of "Bildung" is followed through the stages of illusion and fall to recognition of guilt and insight.

## ACKNOWLEDGMENTS

The persons to whom I am mostly indebted are Professors Egon Schwarz and Liselotte Dieckmann of the Department of Germanic Languages and Literatures at Washington University, St. Louis. The advice and counsel they gave me were invaluable in the compilation of this study. I also thank the many colleagues and friends who supported me during this endeavor.

The institutions which supported me are Washington University, St. Louis, where I studied, and Luther College of Decorah, Iowa, where I teach. The library facilities of the Bayerische Staatsbibliothek, München, and of the University of California were used extensively during the research.

# TABLE OF CONTENTS

# INTRODUCTION

The Bildungsroman is a familiar concept in German literature, but, to my knowledge, the word "Bildungsdrama" has never been used as a literary term. Perhaps that is because of the seeming contradiction in the word itself. "Bildung" implies time, time necessary for a person to mature, and most drama takes place in a matter of hours or at most, days. Even drama that covers a longer period of historical time is limited in stage time. It therefore seems unlikely that the dramatic hero could undergo anything as complex as a "Bildungsprozess" in the short time span covered by the drama. Nevertheless, there is a type of drama for which the designation "Bildungsdrama" is appropriate. This drama came into being at the same time as the Bildungsroman, i.e. in the last part of the eighteenth century, as the Storm and Stress poets emerged from their rebellious youth and sought restore the drama to its classical heritage. One of the first signs of the changing attitude of these poets was to be found in a new image of the young hero. After he had been presented in the Storm and Stress drama in his unrestrained adolescence, the figure of the Young Man began to undergo a maturation process. In the "Bildungsdrama" this process forms the substance of the dramatic plot.

Much has been written about Schiller's DON CARLOS, Goethe's TORQUATO TASSO and Kleist's PRINZ FRIEDRICH VON HOMBURG separately, but no one has ever noted the many similarities among the plays, both historical and thematic, which would suggest grouping them under the heading "Bildungsdrama." Occasionally the "Entwicklungs"- or "Erziehungs"- qualities in the plays have been recognized on an individual basis. Bernhard Blume even uses the term "Erziehungsdrama" in referring to PRINZ FRIED- RICH VON HOMBURG,[1] but the plays have never been discussed collectively and in historical perspective as counterparts to a "Bildungsroman"-form.

In introducing the term "Bildung" in connection with the drama, we do not mean that the hero's experience is necessarily good. The term "Bildung" in connection with the drama is not supposed to suggest that the hero necessarily becomes better than he was, or that he is initially an imperfect human being and must be improved upon. The authors are depicting first of all an unavoidable growth process, a loss of innocence, in the settings in which these heroes are cast. But in addition there is sufficient evidence to believe that the authors also see a justice in this growth process. As it turns out, these three plays all represent a turning point in the authors' lives. They were all written as the authors

---

[1] Berhard Blume, for example, writes: "wenn es neben dem Erziehungs- oder Entwicklungsroman so etwas wie ein Erziehungsdrama gibt, dann ist der Homburg eins." ("Kleist und Goethe," *Heinrich von Kleist. Aufsätze und Essays*, ed. Walter Müller-Seidel (Darmstadt, 1967), p. 176.)

themselves were leaving youth behind them, and for the first time their heroes face a reality that is given equal consideration to the hero's own claims. The authors intentionally place their heroes in a situation where they must eventually accept the superiority, and the *righteousness,* of a reality outside of themselves. There is an ethical tendency in each play which explains the use of the word "Bildung."

Character development in the drama necessarily proceeds rapidly, and the hero's "Bildung" takes place quickly in the space of one brief moment, the moment of insight. Käte Hamburger, in her book, *Die Logik der Dichtung,* provides theoretical evidence that "Bildung" may well be the subject of the drama as well as the novel. By showing that the drama and the novel derive their meaning from the same basic structural principles, i.e. from a plot which can have to do with any aspect of reality, Miss Hamburger establishes the internal possibility for the existence of a "Bildungsdrama."[2] The main distinguishing features between the "Bildungsdrama" and the "Bildungsroman" are concentration of plot, limitation of experience, and the rapidity with which the character growth takes place. As in the novel, the dramatic hero learns primarily from life itself, although there are leadership figures present.

---

[2] Käte Hamburger writes: "Der letzte allgemeinste Sinn des Symbolcharakters jeder Fiktion bedeutet nichts anderes als die von der Wirklichkeit und damit auch von der Wirklichkeitsbeschreibung, d.i. vom Aussagesystem abgetrennte, in sich geschlossene Struktur, in der alle Einzelteile und -motive aufeinander zugeordnet sind, kurz nichts dem Zufall oder besser der Willkür unterworfen ist, der die Wirklichkeit selbst ausgesetzt ist. Diese Forderung ist für das Drama meist strenger erhoben worden als für den Roman, der gerade darum von der klassischen Ästhetik (Hegels und Vischers) getadelt wurde, weil er sich zu sehr der Wirklichkeit des Lebens, der "prosaischen Weltordnung" anschmiege. Dennoch hat das Drama in diesem Punkte keine andere Struktur als der Roman; nur die Konzentration der Handlung auf die Aufführung lässt hier dieses Gesetz stärker hervortreten. Sowohl die dramatische wie die epische Mimesis ist gleichbedeutend mit dem Entworfensein der Handlung, und das ist mit der Handlung selbst. Ihr symbolischer Sinn kann sehr eng an den irgendeiner Wirklichkeit angeschmiegt sein und besteht dann oftmals darin, eine besondere Eigenschaft des betreffenden Wirklichkeitsstoffes 'realistisch' herauszuarbeiten: einen sozialen oder einen psychologischen auf irgendein Lebensverhältnis, einen Charakter bezüglichen und dergleichen mehr." (*Die Logik der Dichtung* (Stuttgart, 1968), 275−76.)

Chapter 1:
# THE EMERGENCE OF THE YOUNG MAN AS DRAMATIC HERO

It is interesting, and in this study it is necessary, to trace the image of the Young Man as dramatic hero, as it developed in German literature in the eighteenth century. The three plays, DON CARLOS, TORQUATO TASSO and PRINZ FRIEDRICH VON HOMBURG, will be discussed both separately and together from many points of departure, and the plays should be placed in historical context in order to show the reasons for their selection in writing about a particular kind of Young Man image.

The eighteenth century was a time of reaction against traditional forms and ways of thinking. With the emancipation of the individual during the Age of Enlightenment, people started to question the ideas handed down to them by many kinds of practical and intellectual authority. They began by challenging the very concept of themselves as sinful creatures dependent on the Church for eternal salvation. They started to think of themselves as preferred beings, who, in their power of reason and gift of free will, had been given the ability to determine their own destiny and to provide for their own spiritual welfare. They no longer viewed themselves as innately wicked creatures, but began to believe that it was possible to better themselves in this life and to approach a state of human perfection. This led them to an increased interest in the question of ethics, which remained one of their chief concerns throughout the century. The methods of defining the "good" differed with the particular age, but the underlying belief in the inherent goodness and perfectibility of the human race remained unchanged. It was this new concept which formed the basis of the humanistic idealism of the Age of Goethe, in which the figure of the Young Man came to play an important part. Through his character and development as revealed in various literary forms, the poets found one means of expressing their faith in the individual's potential.

The drama did not remain immune to the questioning spirit of the century. Immediately following the great period of French neo-classical tragedy in the Age of Louis XIV, various reactions set in, partially in an attempt to free the drama from aristocratic authority. The way for the appearance of the young hero on the stage was paved in the domestic tragedy, which came into being around 1730 in England as a protest against the traditional concept of tragedy. Audiences were outgrowing the idea that the tragic hero had to belong to the upper classes and they were ready for something new. It had always been important, in order to satisfy Aristotle's requirement for tragic effect, that the tragic hero belong to the aristocracy. This rule had been carefully preserved again in the French drama of the preceding century. As part of the new century's rejection of traditional forms, the English poets introduced the middle-class hero into their dramas, thereby creating an entirely new concept of tragedy, which was soon to be brought into Germany by Lessing in MISS SARA SAMPSON. The precedent for something new in the drama had thus already been established when the Storm and Stress poets emerged with their image of the young hero.

For the rationalists in the early eighteenth century, the way to moral perfection had lain in the power of reason. Lessing's treatise on DIE ERZIEHUNG DES MENSCHENGESCHLECHTS, although of an advanced date, can be called a summary of this type of thinking. Not so much as a reaction to, but rather as a contemporary but separate movement along with this emphasis on rational powers, the Storm and Stress generation soon appeared on the scene. This "new chapter of the Enlightenment"[1] was at one with the rationalists' efforts to free people from authoritarian control and to put the responsibility for the direction of their lives into their own hands, but it proceeded towards its goals in a different way. Storm and Stress believed not in reason, which it viewed as simply another restriction on its person, but in the emotions, the natural instincts, as the means by which a person could reach his fullest potential. The Storm and Stress movement expanded the "Empfindsamkeit" of the Pietist movement and the middle-class drama into the idea of "Gefühl." Through feeling, through obedience to nothing more than the voice of the heart, it held that one could first arrive at true freedom. All sides of the person had to be liberated and one had to live in complete accordance with nature in order to achieve full humanity.

The Storm and Stress movement of the 1770's was a literary movement of decisive importance in the history of German literature and especially in the further development of the drama. Lessing, only a few years earlier, had given the German drama its first respectability as a national genre, and now it was left to the next generation to give it the new impetus which sent it along its path to greatness. The introduction of the Young Man as dramatic hero did much to contribute to this greatness. Taking Shakespeare as their model, the young Storm and Stress authors endeavored first of all, as had the English authors and Lessing before them, to free the drama from the yoke of neo-classicism which had held sway over it for more than a century. They thought they recognized in Shakespeare a call to native genius and a repudiation of all artificial rules and decorum. One of the first traditions which they attacked was the one which expected the tragic hero to be a man already exposed to the world and established in his life's pattern. It had always been believed that only a person who had something to lose could be a potentially tragic figure, and a young man as yet uninitiated into life did not meet this requirement. The Storm and Stress

---

1   The first section of the Introduction to: *Sturm und Drang – Ein Lesebuch für unsere Zeit,* eds. Klaus Hermann and Joachim Müller (Berlin and Weimar, 1967) is entitled "Ein neuer Abschnitt der Aufklärung."

poets, in their protest against traditional authority, rejected this idea and introduced a young man like themselves as the protagonist of their dramas. They used him as spokesman for the idea of natural existence, as opposed to existence based on tradition and reason. Heeding Rousseau's call to return to nature, they condemned all aspects of society which for them constituted a violation of nature and a repression of individual human freedom, and the new image of the young hero served as the instrument of their protest. For the most part the literary result was poor, because of meager talent and too many other broken rules. The two men who proved to have great talent, Goethe and Schiller, did succeed in producing several effective plays during this period, and it might be worth investigating how it was possible that a very young person with nothing but his youth and idealism to speak for him could suddenly become an interesting stage figure.

The "young men" portrayed in the Storm and Stress dramas were men of feeling, acting solely according to their natural inclination without any regard for the laws or customs of their environment. Some were completely disillusioned with life and saw no reason whatsoever for living.[2] Others found their purpose in pursuing personal freedom as an ideal in itself,[3] and still others pursued freedom in a larger context as a struggle against some unjust aspect of society. Leisewitz' Julius of Tarent is engaged in this latter kind of struggle. Julius belongs to a royal family, but he spurns all social convention by abandoning the duty to his heritage for the love of a middle-class girl. He has no consideration for the claims of his father's world, he refuses to listen to the reasonable arguments of his older friend, Aspermonte, and he gives no thought to renouncing his love to accept his duties as crown prince of Tarent. His claims are presented sympathetically in comparison to those of his brother, Guido, who knows how to conform, and Julius' tragic fate brings about the end of the family. There is no attempt at reconciliation or accommodation between the two worlds because, as presented by the author, there is no question that Julius is in the right. Julius is typical of most Storm and Stress heroes. Action is dictated by unrestrained feeling and no rational considerations are allowed to stand in the way of personal freedom. There is thus little or no character development in the hero. He remains essentially the same person from beginning to end, stubbornly persisting in his state of illusion until fate gets the better of him and he falls.

---

[2] Grimaldi of Klinger's ZWILLINGE is an example of an eighteenth-century youth suffering from "Weltschmerz." Life has lost all meaning for him since he lost his love, and he does nothing but bemoan his lot and hope for an early death.

[3] Goethe's Clavigo insists on living his own life to the point of refusing to marry the girl to whom he is engaged.

While most of the "young man" figures in Storm and Stress drama end without any insight at all, Karl Moor is an exception who should be discussed. Moor, a student grieving in the belief that his father has disowned him, leads a band of robbers and takes it upon himself to reform society according to his own ideals. He robs and plunders with complete abandon, taking from the rich and giving to the poor, all the time thinking nobly of himself in the conviction that society's unfair structure justifies his deeds. Finally he sees that his course of action is about to destroy society instead of improving it, and that, in spite of his good intentions, all he is doing is trying to correct one injustice with another injustice. At this moment he repents and gives himself up to the law as a means of atonement. This action takes place in the final moments of the play and almost as an afterthought. In reaching an understanding about the folly of his hubris and admitting his guilt, Karl Moor is a forerunner of our three heroes. What distinguishes DIE RÄUBER from the "Bildungsdrama" of the later period is the fact that Moor reaches his final insight on his own initiative and as a secondary "coup de théâtre" to the poet's main purpose of showing the workings of unleashed feeling, whereas in our "Bildungsdrama" the hero is guided by other characters throughout the play and his ultimate understanding is the main intent of the dramatic action.

The changing image of the Young Man was one of the first signs that Goethe and Schiller were leaving their Storm and Stress youth behind them. As these two gifted poets matured and made their own adjustments to society, it was inevitable that their poetic creations would change with them. This happened not only in the drama, but also in the novel as the difference between WERTHER and WILHELM MEISTER demonstrates. The changing views of the poets were reflected first of all in the fact that something positive began to emerge from the young hero's conflict with society. Instead of the purely tragic endings of the Storm and Stress dramas, the new hero begins to reach some sort of understanding about himself and the world, which, if it does not completely avert the tragedy, at least mitigates it. In other words, instead of experiencing only periods of illusion and fall, as the Storm and Stress hero had done, the new hero progresses further to a final redeeming insight. It is this insight which, more than anything else, forms the common bond among our three dramas and distinguishes them from the dramas of the earlier period.[4] True, the Storm and

---

[4]  Kleist, of course, has no direct historical relationship to Storm and Stress. An analogy to Storm and Stress can be made within Kleist's own life, however, and that is done in the following chapter where the PRINCE OF HOMBURG is discussed as a transitional drama in Kleist's works. The PRINCE OF HOMBURG occupies the same position, as a product of Kleist's emergence from his "Storm and Stress" youth, as do CARLOS and TASSO in Schiller's and Goethe's lives.

Stress hero must have reached some degree of awareness when he fell, for if nothing else he had to see that he had failed in his intentions. But the new hero does much more, he not only realizes that he has fallen, but he understands *why* he has fallen. He comprehends what it was in himself and in the world about him, and in his relationship to this world, that caused his fall, and this comprehension makes it easier for him to accept his fate. What the new hero then does with this knowledge once he has it is of secondary importance to the fact that the knowledge is reached.

The new hero is thus no longer portrayed as an unbridled "Gefühlsmensch" from beginning to end, but begins to undergo a maturation process which makes him capable of accommodation. Still a passionate young man of feeling at the start, he is, through a variety of influences, ultimately transformed into a spiritually enlightened and temperamentally sobered individual. This character growth takes place in a world which the hero treats antagonistically, but in contrast to the Storm and Stress dramas, the outside world is now given a validity of its own and its claims are given some consideration. The purpose of the new drama is to bring the hero to a recognition of reality and to reach some accommodation between the two worlds, and the hero's insight is the manifestation of this objective.

A later chapter is devoted to the configuration of the "teachers" in our three "Bildungsdramen." Here we point out only that another way in which the new plays differ from the Storm and Stress plays is in their "teacher" figures, a male antagonist and a beloved woman in each, who work actively to bring about a change in the young man. The Storm and Stress dramas naturally did not have or need these figures in them, for it was not the intention that the young man learn to adjust himself to the antagonistic world. Both the male and female figures in our "Bildungsdramen" represent an opposite order of things into which the young man is initiated by the dramatic action.

A German drama of the same period which also has a teacher-student relationship in it, and which should be discussed in developing our theme, is Goethe's IPHIGENIE. The heroine, Iphigenie, is the embodiment of the ideal of pure humanity. In Iphigenie, inclination and duty merge into complete harmony, the voice of the heart extolled by the Storm and Stress generation becomes the voice of conscience, and it is this purity in Iphigenie which enables her to free her brother Orest from the curse which possesses him and to restore him to normal health. Orest's restoration is a healing process rather than a maturation process; he never lives in a state of happy illusion from which experience must free him. Except for brief moments of contentment and hope with his friend, Pylades, Orest lives under the shadow of his disastrous heritage and deed, believing that his guilt has doomed him to tragedy. Under Iphigenie's purifying influence he finally confesses his guilt and is able to cast off his delusions. There is no willful self-conquest on Orest's part. It is the sanctifying presence of his sister alone which brings about his conversion. In contrast to our other heroes, Orest is conscious of his guilt from the start, and it is the liberation from guilt, rather than the recognition of it, which determines his inner renewal.

An important forerunner to IPHIGENIE in the idea of "Humanität," and also a drama with a strong teacher-student pattern, is Lessing's NATHAN DER WEISE. Nathan is the first figure in German literature who proclaims the idea of pure humanity, and like Iphigenie, he influences through example. When the young Templar first meets Nathan, he is an unsympathetic Antisemite who is almost sorry that he has saved a Jew from death. Through Nathan's wise and selfless image, and his persistent attitude of tolerance toward the Templar, the Templar himself assimilates these qualities to his own being and is transformed into an enlightened and purified person. It is significant to our contention of "Bildung" in drama that already here, in this "Meisterwerk der Aufklärung," there exists a basic pattern of dramatic tension between teacher and student.

Before we begin the discussion of the plays as such, we should summarize why just these three dramas, CARLOS, TASSO, and the PRINCE OF HOMBURG, are chosen to illustrate the idea of "Bildungsdrama" in German literature. If character growth in the young hero is a general trend of the time, why do we not, for example, consider Orest and the Templar in detail, or include in the investigation a young man like Max Piccolomini, who also conquers himself. And what is the justification for including the PRINCE OF HOMBURG, which was written some years later than CARLOS and TASSO, and historically has no direct relationship to Storm and Stress. First of all, in order to demonstrate the existence of a "genre," it would be necessary to include as many examples as could be grouped and discussed meaningfully together. These three plays not only have the "young man" theme in common, but are structurally so alike — court, antagonists, beloved women — that much of the exposition can be done for all three simultaneously. Secondly, and more importantly, only these three heroes, of all the young heroes of the time, undergo a maturation process as the essence of the dramatic plot. Only Carlos, Tasso, and the Prince of Homburg are both major stage figures and the title heroes of their respective plays, and only these three young men proceed to insight as the main goal of the dramatic action and as the main intention of their authors.

## Chapter 2:
## THE SIMILARITIES OF ORIGIN OF THE THREE PLAYS

To trace the genesis of DON CARLOS is to substantiate much of what has been said in the first chapter. Schiller wrote the play between 1783 and 1787. These four years constitute a transitional period in which his ideas concerning the role of the title hero changed considerably. In the original prose version, which was still very much "Storm and Stress" in character, Carlos was not to be the object of a "Bildungsprozess." Schiller's purpose was simply to portray a tragic love story, "ein Familiengemälde in einem fürstlichen Hause,"[1] and Carlos and Elisabeth were to be the victims of an inhuman state system, where natural feeling was sacrificed to political expediency and to the demands of the Church's inquisition. In this first version, stress was placed on the right of natural feeling to assert itself, the same theme which had been the subject of Schiller's earlier plays, and here Elisabeth was allowed to return Carlos' love. The intention was that the lovers would eventually conquer their passion, not with any help from outside, but as the result of inner struggle, much in the same manner as Karl Moor finally conquers himself or as Luise Miller renounces her love for Ferdinand. In the first version, Posa was relegated to the position of Carlos' friend and confidante to the lovers, and his sacrificial death was to occur only out of friendship for Carlos.

As the scope of the drama widened and the political ideas took precedence for Schiller over the themes of love and friendship, Posa's role became more significant and Carlos was forced to find a new purpose. It now became Schiller's intention, in order to depict his new ideas, to have Carlos undergo a maturation process at the hands of his friend. In the final version, Carlos progresses from an uncontained youth, temporarily blinded by his love for Elisabeth, to a man who conquers his emotions and clarifies his thoughts, and who concerns himself with the humanitarian causes promoted by Posa. In this last version, Carlos also conquers his love, but with Posa's help, and not simply as an act of renunciation, but in order that he might be able to accept his higher calling in life. Posa, through whom Schiller proclaims his new ideals of human freedom, becomes a "teacher" to Carlos, educating him to the importance of these ideals and thus preparing him for his future role as king. Posa's death then becomes the final means by which Carlos is freed from his passion and raised to the stature of his noble birth.

---

[1] Letter to Dalberg of June 7, 1784.

Schiller tells in the BRIEFE ÜBER DON CARLOS how his interest gradually shifted from Carlos to Posa over the years, as the new ideas began to occupy his mind:

> Während der Zeit nämlich, dass ich es ausarbeitete, welches mancher Unterbrechungen wegen eine ziemlich lange Zeit war, hat sich — in mir selbst vieles verändert .... Neue Ideen, die indes bei mir aufkamen, verdrängten die frühern; Carlos selbst war in meiner Gunst gefallen, vielleicht aus keinem andern Grunde, als weil ich ihm in Jahren zu weit vorausgesprungen war, und aus der entgegengesetzten Ursache hatte Marquis Posa seinen Platz eingenommen.[2]

It was to be expected that Posa and not Carlos should become the exponent of the new "Humanitätsideen." Carlos was too young and inexperienced for such a role, and besides, as Gerhard Storz points out, his position as direct antagonist to the king on the personal level made it impossible for him to become the messenger of a political ideology as well:

> Dramatische Bewegung konnte sich aus der Botschaft von einer 'reineren, sanfteren Humanität' nur dann ergeben, wenn eine Figur, die dem König gegenüber innerhalb des Handlungsgefüges von mehr neutraler Stellung war als Carlos, sie an den König richtete.[3]

Posa, the wiser of the two, and by nature more politically oriented than Carlos, was Schiller's logical choice to become the spokesman of his new ideas.

Because of the apparent vacillation between Carlos and Posa as dramatic hero, Schiller has sometimes been accused of inconsistency in his play. Such a large change of focus from one character to another, as Schiller admits to, could not help but leave its mark on the play's structure. For Schiller, there is no breach of purpose, however. He continues on in the BRIEFE to defend Carlos as title hero because, although Posa became the embodiment of the political message of the play, Carlos' orientation to that political message forms the unifying element of the plot.[4] A combination of democratic ideals and the effort to accept those ideals as the basis for one's life is, according to Schiller, the substance of DON CARLOS. Schiller states that it was not his purpose as part of the plot to first instill the political ideas in Carlos — that had already occurred in advance of the enacted drama. Schiller's aim was to show these ideas in conflict with unhappy passion and then to reaffirm them by allowing them to emerge victoriously in a typically Schiller-like struggle between inclination and duty, all the more invulnerable because of the test they had been put to. Schiller emphasizes that it

---

2  Erster Brief.
3  Gerhard Storz, "Die Struktur des Don Carlos," *Jahrbuch der Schillergesellschaft*, 4 (1960), p. 129.
4  Achter und neunter Brief.

was not his intention to have Carlos ready to assume his noble calling at the beginning of the play, but rather that it was the purpose of the play to develop his character to that point:

> Ein weiches, wohlwollendes Herz, Enthusiasmus für das Grosse und Schöne, Delikatesse, Mut, Standhaftigkeit, uneigennützige Grossmut sollte er besitzen, schöne und helle Blicke des Geistes sollte er zeigen, aber *weise* sollte er nicht sein. Der künftige grosse Mann sollte in ihm schlummern, aber ein feuriges Blut sollte ihm jetzt noch nicht erlauben, es wirklich zu sein. Alles, was den trefflichen Regenten macht, alles, was die Erwartungen seines Freundes und die Hoffnungen einer auf ihn harrenden Welt rechtfertigen kann, alles, was sich vereinigen muss, sein vorgesetztes Ideal von einem künftigen Staat auszuführen, sollte sich in diesem Charakter beisammen finden: aber entwickelt sollte es noch nicht sein, noch nicht von Leidenschaft geschieden, noch nicht zu reinem Golde geläutert. Darauf kam es ja eigentlich erst an, ihn dieser Vollkommenheit näher zu bringen, die ihm jetzt noch mangelt; ein mehr vollendeter Charakter des Prinzen hätte mich des ganzen Stücks überhoben.[5]

From Schiller's own evaluation one can conclude that Schiller, himself, considered DON CARLOS to be a "Bildungsdrama." Carlos' character growth is the thread which holds all parts of the action together, and when viewed in this light, Schiller insists, any seeming inconsistencies vanish, and the play emerges as a logically developed whole.[6]

It is in Schiller's dramatic work as a whole that one can best see the changing image of the young hero, and Carlos is the first of his heroes to undergo a growth process. The play appeared in the same year as IPHIGENIE and it was greatly influenced by NATHAN. With CARLOS, Schiller turns away from the middle-class tragedy and seeks to raise the drama to a higher plane. His introduction of verse form as the dramatic medium, and the choice of historic setting are two external signs of this. In CARLOS, the attempt to flee society is

---

[5] *Ibid.,* neunter Brief.

[6] André von Gronicka ("Friedrich Schiller's Marquis Posa: A Character Study," *Germanic Review,* 26 (1951), 196–214) disagrees with this evaluation. In his opinion, Schiller's assertion that Carlos' character development is the unifying theme of the play is insufficient because, first of all, "such an explanation fails to take into account Schiller's testimony that Posa had displaced Carlos as the key figure." and secondly, "this explanation fails to justify the tragic ending of the work." "Neither in Carlos' initial character nor in his subsequent development, crowned as it is with success at the very moment of his arrest, can we find sufficient cause, from either the aesthetic or the ethic point of view, for his or Posa's doom." Von Gronicka believes that Posa must be viewed as the central figure of the play, for the tragedy, the outcome of the work, is the result of Posa's character: "Once we accept Posa, the despot of the idea, as the key figure of the tragedy, its artistic and ideational unity becomes immediately apparent. In Posa we have the character with the tragic flaw which furnishes sufficient cause for the final catastrophe; moreover, through him, his attitude and resultant fate, Schiller spells out his central unifying message which is best summed up in his own words: 'nichts führt zum *Guten,* was nicht *natürlich* ist.' " (all quotes from page 211).

changed — although still with a tragic outcome — into the attempt to better the human lot. Rousseau's call to return to nature, which formed the background of the Storm and Stress hero's struggle against society, has been replaced by the effort to reform society. Carlos and Posa are still pitted against Philipp's world, but their ideal of freedom advances beyond Karl Moor's ideal in the sense that it is less personal and has a universal purpose. The method of accomplishing the ideal is also more refined. Although Posa is still capable of raw revolution, as his precautionary military measures show, he thinks politically and would prefer to reach his goal by political maneuver. Beginning with Carlos, Schiller's heroes seek an inner harmony with themselves to compensate for the inevitability of their outer fate. They want to cope with the outside world through self-clarification. Both Carlos and Posa finally secure an inner freedom which wins at least a moral victory over the tyranny of Spanish rule. Carlos never succumbs to his environment in the same way that Karl Moor, Fiesco, or Ferdinand fell victim to their surroundings. Although there is still much "Storm and Stress" in Carlos, he is not as uncompromising as Schiller's earlier heroes and therefore he is less vulnerable. Carlos experiences three crises in the play, each of which he conquers, the first two with help, the last one alone. Adolf Beck has shown how Carlos is the first of Schiller's heroes who preserves his humanity in the face of the personal despair which accompanies a loss of trust in another person.[7] Carlos maintains a degree of purity throughout the play, and finally he achieves an inner victory over his outwardly tragic fate.

This change in Schiller's presentation of his heroes took place as the poet himself moved qway from the captivity of his younger years to the freedom of Bauerbach and Dresden.[8] Beginning at this time, Schiller's intellectual struggle for human freedom no longer seemed doomed to failure. He began to discover ways to preserve personal freedom within the restrictions of society. As the poet began to view the problem of human freedom more objectively, the emphasis in his writings shifted from outward defeat to inner spiritual victory. The change of outlook had already existed in the Bauerbach version of CARLOS, where Carlos was also eventually to conquer himself and his love. As Schiller's interest moved to political involvement, Carlos' individual fate became subordinated to the higher question of freedom for humanity.

Another indication of Schiller's poetic development is seen in a milder portrayal of the antagonist. Although it is obvious in CARLOS that Schiller still stands on his hero's side, for the first time the opposition, too, is presented with

---

[7]  Adolf Beck, "Die Krise des Menschen im Drama des jungen Schiller." *Forschung und Deutung* (Bonn, 1966), esp. p. 157f.

[8]  Compare: Melitta Gerhard, *Schiller* (Bern, 1950), p. 97f.

some degree of sympathy. Philipp is not completely evil, but is endowed with human qualities which elicit the viewer's interest and, at times, even his compassion. He has also been accorded a central position in the drama, as Schiller himself explains:

> Wenn dieses Trauerspiel schmelzen soll, so muss es — wie mich deucht — durch die Situation und den Charakter des König Philipps geschehen. Auf der Wendung, die man diesem gibt, ruht vielleicht das ganze Gewicht der Tragödie . . . . Man erwartet — ich weiss nicht welches? Ungeheuer, sobald von Philipp dem Zweiten die Rede ist — mein Stück fällt zusammen, sobald man ein solches darin findet.

This statement, which appeared in the preface to the first version of Act I published in the *Rheinische Thalia* in March, 1785, shows that Schiller, early in the composition of the play, intended to lessen the hostility formerly assigned to the outside world in order to deepen the background for the hero's struggle and inner triumph.

Not only has the antagonist been given more consideration, but now for the first time the hero shares a major part of the responsibility for his undoing. Schiller's main reason for writing the BRIEFE was to explain Posa's part in his own tragedy, and Carlos' "Bildungsprozess" is for the purpose of correcting a weakness in Carlos' nature that Schiller censures. Schiller does not permit Carlos to disregard the responsibilities of his noble heritage. He gives these responsibilities precedence over Carlos' love for Elisabeth, requiring that the love be conquered so that the responsibilities can be accepted. Philipp is still the villain in the dramatic involvement, but for the first time the hero is largely guilty, too.

There are some facts about the way in which Goethe's TASSO developed historically that are relevant to our image of the young hero emerging from Storm and Stress. It ist noteworthy that TASSO, like CARLOS, was fashioned over such a long period of time, nine years to be exact, that, like in DON CARLOS, a change in the author himself is noticeable in the work. TASSO, like CARLOS, suffers from an apparent break in the middle, where the antagonist seems to become dearer to the poet than the hero, and there are other inconsistencies and residuals of this time problem.[9] It is unfortunate for the historical consideration of TASSO that nothing remains of the UR-TASSO, and that all attempts to reconstruct it from the only extant version of the play, no matter how ingenious these attempts may be,[10] are nothing more than pure hypotheses. It would help if one could say with certainty that the drama as Goethe originally conceived it was still to have been a Storm and Stress work;

---

[9] For a searching discussion of the inconsistencies in TASSO, see: Walter Silz, "Ambivalences in Goethe's TASSO," *Germanic Review,* 31 (1956), 243–68.

[10] Compare, for example, Hans M. Wolff's chapter on TASSO in his book: *Goethes Weg zur Humanität* (München, 1951), 66–101.

that, as in WERTHER, the artist's problem was to have been presented from his side alone with no allowance for the outside world, and that the final tragedy was to have resulted from the poet's collision against an intriguing, tyrannical court, with no mitigating insight on his part and with no accommodation considered or attempted. Then one could document once again in a single example how the image of the young hero, this time specifically the creative artist, changed as the poet himself matured. As it is, one must be content with the evidence of WERTHER,[11] and satisfied with speculation as far as TASSO is concerned. But speculation here is rather valid. For most critics, Antonio, after Act Two, represents an accommodation by Goethe to reflect his own matured self after the Italy experience and the intervening administrative years at the Weimar court. Liselotte Blumenthal has shown by her examination of the TASSO manuscript[12] that Goethe did indeed change his mind about Antonio's role in the course of composition, and that he was intent on presenting him in an ever more favorable light. It is also interesting that Karl August praised the final version of the play, but disapproved of the first.[13] We know that when Goethe picked up the work at the end of his Italian journey, he was disheartened to discover that he could no longer use what he had written in his early Weimar days: "Tasso muss umgearbeitet werden; was da steht, ist zu nichts zu brauchen."[14] Either Goethe had come upon new source material which refuted his original impression of Tasso, or he himself had changed so much in the interval that his former values concerning the play were no longer acceptable for him. With Goethe still in his developing years as far as his poetry is concerned, and considering the scope of his genius and his aptitude for change, the latter possibility is surely the more likely one.[15] Whatever the case, the artist's conflict with society as presented in the final version of TASSO is no longer one-sided. The outside world has now attained a validity of its own, and its claims are represented with equal strength to the poet's.[16] The tragedy does not result from

---

[11] In the years between the conception and the completion of TASSO, Goethe undertook to write a second version of WERTHER, in which he hoped, to quote E. L. Stahl: "to give a more objective presentation of Werther's sufferings as well as of Albert's character and role in the novel." (Introduction to *Tasso* (Oxford, 1962), p. XVII).

[12] In: *Goethe,* neue Folge des Jahrbuchs der Goethegesellschaft, 12 (1950), p. 105.

[13] In a letter from Rome to Karl August of March 28, 1788, Goethe writes: "Hätte ich es nicht angefangen, so würde ich es jetzt nicht wählen, und ich erinnere mich wohl noch, dass Sie mir davon abrieten."

[14] Note from Rome of February 1, 1788.

[15] We do know that Goethe read the first scholarly biography of Tasso, that of Serassi, in Rome in March, 1788 (letter to Karl August of March 28, 1788, quoted above), from which he borrowed much information for the revised TASSO, but that would not explain his statement made at the beginning of February.

[16] Perhaps this is the reason why Goethe once called Tasso "ein gesteigerter Werther." As E. L. Stahl writes in his Introduction to *Tasso* (cited above): "TORQUATO TASSO is 'ein gesteigerter Werther' not least because the drama contains a balanced polarity between

evil intrigue or from a blind refusal on the part of the artist to adjust to the demands of "life," but from well-meaning attempts on both sides to bridge a gap which, in Tasso's case, remains unbridgeable. TASSO is a personal testimony of Goethe's own life at Weimar, and of his dilemma as a poet performing as a statesman at court. Whereas Goethe, the genius, the man of both worlds, finally was able to reconcile the conflict in himself, Tasso, the pure poet, ist unable to do so, and his recognition of this fact at the end of the play forms the major part of his insight. Like WERTHER, TASSO is a confession of the artist at odds with the world, but unlike Werther, this artist does not end by destroying himself. Although the play ends tragically, Tasso ultimately realizes his mistake and reaches a degree of self-knowledge if not self-acceptance which tends to lessen the impact.

Goethe had a way of ridding himself of his personal problems through his poetry. It is well-known that he once called his writings "Bruchstücke einer grossen Konfession." When, following his separation from Weimar and his residence in Italy, Goethe saw, at least in his own life, the necessity for the artist to make concessions to the world in which he lives, he was able to sublimate his conflict by giving it poetic expression in TASSO, just as earlier he had been able to outlive the "Werther-Krankheit" by writing the novel. Tasso falls, that Goethe might adjust to his life in Weimar, the same way that Werther had committed suicide, that the author could overcome his own love affair and move on to the next chapter of his life. Thus one can say that Goethe experienced a "Bildungsprozess" in himself through his creative works, and the Storm and Stress transition, while not as demonstrable in TASSO as in CARLOS, is nonetheless apparent.

It has frequently been asserted that Goethe's philosophy prevented him from ever writing a pure tragedy. FAUST, Goethe's greatest work, and his most potentially tragic work, ends favorably for the hero, in contrast to earlier versions of the legend, precisely because Goethe saw something redeemable about Faust in the fact of his striving alone. TASSO, for all its tragic import, leaves a note of hope that under more favorable circumstances the poet might surmount his problem and find a niche in the real world. Wolfdietrich Rasch makes the point that, in spite of the unmistakably tragic nature of the drama, Goethe's message does not lie ultimately in Tasso's downfall, but in his insight. According to Rasch, there is no question that Goethe is demanding the reconciliation of the poet and society: "So tief und so unlösbar im TASSO der tragische Zwiespalt erscheint, so unverkennbar ist doch darin zu spüren, dass Goethe selbst die Versöhnung zwischen Dichter und Gesellschaft forderte und

Tasso and Antonio which the earlier novel lacked by its one-sided presentation of the chief characters." (XVII) (Goethe's idea of 'Steigerung,' as E. M. Wilkinson has shown, is closely linked to the meaning of the word 'Polarität.' ["Tasso – ein gesteigerter Werther in the Light of Goethe's Principle of Steigerung," *Modern Language Review,* 44 (1949), 305–28].

für notwendig hielt.[17] There is also evidence in the structure of the drama to support the idea that Goethe's chief goal was Tasso's insight. When one considers that the embrace scene, where Tasso's tragedy reaches its climax, is structurally still part of the poet's fall, and that the fall continues on in the blasphemy scene, then the only real turning point in Tasso's development is his final insight.

Kleist's PRINZ FRIEDRICH VON HOMBURG was written some twenty years later than CARLOS and TASSO, and there are no historical parallels to be drawn between this play and the Age of Storm and Stress. An analogy to the origins of CARLOS and TASSO can be made in Kleist's own life, however. Kleist has been seen by some critics as a late Storm and Stress "Genie."[18] Like Goethe and Schiller, he spent the first years of his poetic existence extolling feeling as the only valid criterion for living. His early heroes, up to and including Penthesilea, all rise and fall by this one behavioral standard. The Prince is the first of Kleist's heroes to extend beyond this limit — as J. M. Benson says: "to see his feeling apparently defeated by reality and yet to survive,"[19] and since the PRINCE is Kleist's last play, it is tempting to make the comparison to Goethe and Schiller and say that as Kleist emerged from his Storm and Stress youth, his heroes, too, began to grow. One can also look at Kleist as a romanticist and thus as a natural inheritor of the Storm and Stress philosophy of absolute feeling.

Very little is known about the actual genesis of the PRINCE OF HOMBURG. The same is true of most of Kleist's works. Except for DIE FAMILIE GHONOREZ and DER ZERBROCHENE KRUG, even the original manuscripts of the plays are missing. There is thus no compositional progress to trace as was possible for CARLOS and TASSO. All that is known about the PRINCE OF HOMBURG historically, and even that is the result of the most complex deduction,[20] is that the bulk of the play was written during the winter of 1809—10, and that it was completed in the summer of 1811, shortly before Kleist's death. Kleist, at this time of his life, was possessed by an intense nationalism, and since the apparent theme of the PRINCE is the education of the individual to a respect for the law, the play for many years was thought to be a propaganda piece, similar to the HERMANNSSCHLACHT. Gerhard Fricke greatly broadened the interpretational possibilities with his book, *Gefühl und Schicksal bei Heinrich von Kleist,*[21] but the interpretation of the play still

17  Wolfdietrich Rasch, *Goethes TORQUATO TASSO Die Tragödie des Dichters* (Stuttgart, 1954), p. 25.
18  Compare: H. A. Korff, "Das Dichtertum Heinrich von Kleists." *Zeitschrift für Deutschkunde* (1933), p. 426.
19  "Kleists PRINZ FRIEDRICH VON HOMBURG," *Modern Languages,* 46 (1965), p. 103.
20  Richard Samuel has conducted an exhaustive study of the origin of Kleist's play, published as the Introduction to the text edition according to the Heidelberg manuscript (Berlin: Erich Schmidt Verlag, 1964).
21  Berlin, 1929.

remains highly controversial, and much of the reason for this is that we are limited almost exclusively to the text for our understanding of the work.

Just what *is* Kleist saying in this play? The author's message must be discernable in the play itself, and in the PRINCE'S case, this message is very vague. One never finds out exactly what happens in the Prince psychologically in the important scene with Natalie, and because of this, one never really knows what Kleist is thinking either.[22] The ambiguity of the Prince's insight, plus the scantiness of the historical evidence surrounding the work, make it very difficult to ascertain just how much the PRINCE is related in purpose to our other two dramas. One critic sees in the play a complete return to classical drama,[23] another views it as a monument of existentialist thought;[24] this demonstrates the extremes in interpretational possibilities. One thing is certain, however. The *problem* in the PRINCE is the same problem encountered in our other plays. Here, as in CARLOS and TASSO, the configurational pattern centers around an inexperienced hero and an established order. The hero's fate is to come to terms with his environment, and he *does* come to terms with it, regardless of how it is done. This in itself signals a new direction in Kleist's works. In his earlier compositions, Kleist had never given consideration to the world outside his hero. Reality, or fate, had simply been something that stood in the way of his heroes' goals, which, in spite of their extreme nature, Kleist had always completely identified with. His heroes had fallen, like Akmene, the victims of forces beyond their control. Now, in the PRINCE OF HOMBURG, for the first time the hero's own purpose does not reign supreme, but gives way to a higher order, an order which is not evil, but simply exists as a fact to be reckoned with. The Prince is subjected to sociologial forces which require him ultimately to admit his error and to accept the consequences. Kleist is still sympathetic toward his hero, just as Goethe and Schiller sympathize with their young men, but he also represents the claims of the outside world, and the purpose of the play is not merely to show the tragic collision between the individual and reality, but also to bring the individual to an acceptance of reality. The goal is to establish a harmony between the two sides, and this fact in itself relates the play to its classical predecessors.

[22] Much the same thing can be said of TASSO. It should perhaps be pointed out at this time that it is not this author's purpose to try to give a new or definitve interpretation of the heroes' insights, but that it is enough for the scope of this investigation that insight occurs.

[23] Walter Gausewitz, "Kleist und der Kulturidealismus der Klassik," *Monatshefte,* 53, 5 (October, 1961), 239–54.

[24] Alfred Schlagdenhauffen, *L'univers existentiel de Kleist dans le Prince de Hombourg* (Paris, 1953).

John Gearey's essay[25] is supportive evidence that Kleist's last play marks a break with his earlier writings. Most critics have assumed this because of the play's outline, but here is convincing proof that Kleist's thinking has changed with this play. Gearey is able to show, by comparing various specific examples, how Kleist's attitude toward the Prince is different from what it was toward his other heroes. For the first time, Kleist does not identify completely with his hero, but he stands at a distance from him and shows the negative sides of his character as well. Subjectivity is no longer glorified, but is looked upon critically, and although the Prince strikes one as being still very much a Kleistian hero in that the same characteristics are identifiable in him which are typical of all of Kleist's protagonists, these same characteristics, if examined closely, have quite a different quality about them. For example, when the Prince says the word "gleichviel," it denotes irresponsibility more than it awakens tragic expectation.[26] Gearey believes that Kleist intentionally made the Prince somewhat less pure than his other heroes in order to be able to stand in judgment over him, in order to finally reject his own old self and to come to terms with the world: "Homburg, we sense, is Kleist, but we see also that he is not the present Kleist; rather he appears to be a former self whom the author is looking back on and chastizing for a way of thinking which he knows now to have been wrong."[27] For Gearey, there is no question that Kleist considers the Prince guilty. The purpose of the action is not to establish guilt, but to bring the hero to accept that guilt:

> ... he [Kleist] was concentrating, not on the difficulty of establishing guilt, which had been the almost exclusive preoccupation of his previous works, but on the difficulty of accepting it. This is the area in which his new hero is being tested and about which the drama ultimately will have most to say.[28]

Kleist's heroes have a more difficult time in identifying their reality than do Goethe's or Schiller's heroes. Their world is not as anchored, not as well defined, as the world of German Idealism. Kleist himself would call it a "gebrechliche Welt." Kleist's heroes are mostly unconscious of themselves and their motives. They simply act impulsively, according to their inner feeling, but the problem is that this feeling then leads them astray. They become guilty of an involuntary guilt, for which they must still atone, and which is all the more tragic because of

25 "Character and Idea in PRINZ FRIEDRICH VON HOMBURG," *Germanic Review*, 42 (1967), 276–92.
26 *Ibid.*, p. 279f.
27 *Ibid.*, p. 279.
28 *Ibid.*, p. 278.

its unintentional nature. The Prince is the first of Kleist's heroes who has any real chance to avoid tragedy. First, he is given repeated warnings to desist from his mistaken course, and then, when he does fall, he is given the opportunity to rise again. The Prince is the only one of Kleist's protagonists who reaches some sort of balance between subjective feeling and objective reality, and in so doing escapes destruction.

## Chapter 3:
## HOW THE PLAYS DIFFER

The preceding chapters have sought to establish the historical and, in part, topical links among our three dramas. Now it is time to consider the unique qualities of the plays, the specific ideas behind each hero's "Bildung." The plays are, after all, three distinct works of art, and the author, in each case, had his own special problem in mind. Each hero's character development takes place within a specific setting and for a paricular purpose, and this individual combination marks each play's originality. To be complete, therefore, it is necessary to look at the *dissimilarities* of the plays as well as their similarities.

In DON CARLOS Schiller wrote a political play. The problem here is the collision of the naive idealist with the political world. Two centuries and two lines of political thought stand diametrically opposed to each other in Philipp's 16th century inquisitional Spain and Posa's Enlightenment vision of human freedom. The conflict here evolves among three main characters, Carlos, Posa, and Philipp, and in this triangle Carlos plays mostly a victim's role. The real struggle for political supremacy occurs between Posa and Philipp, and Carlos is a victim of both sides of the struggle. In political leaning, of course, Carlos is on Posa's side, but his betrayal of Posa's political goals in favor of a personal love makes him as much an object of Posa's manipulation as of Philipp's. Carlos' "Bildungsprozess" begins with his clash against his father's world and continues in the direct efforts of his antagonist-friend to regain him for his political mission, which forms the matrix of the play. In Schiller's drama we have two young men against the establishment, and on the political scale Posa represents an advanced stage of Carlos. The purpose of the play is to bring Carlos to Posa's way of thinking politically, to make of the crown prince, as Schiller says, the future "Schöpfer des Menschenglücks."[1]

Carlos learns more from conscious attempts to change him than do either Tasso or the Prince of Homburg. When Schiller turned to the political emphasis in the play's development, Carlos' love for Elisabeth became something undesirable, something that stood in the way of the higher idea and had to be overcome. No longer was the theme to be the unfortunate impossibility of realizing this love because of Philipp, an old "Storm and Stress" theme, but Carlos' love for Elisabeth was from the very beginning regarded as wrong, as an obstacle which had to be surmounted for the sake of "humanity." Both Schiller and Posa share this view and that is why Carlos has so little choice as far as his future is concerned. Not only Philipp, but also Posa works to the destruction of Carlos' love and Carlos is left little self-determination. There is no question that

[1] BRIEFE ÜBER DON CARLOS, neunter Brief.

Carlos' fall is "wrong" and that he must be rehabilitated at all costs. Posa, from the time of his arrival, manipulates Carlos with no feeling at all for Carlos' own interests. Carlos allows this because he feels a conflict about his situation, and also because he loves Posa and needs his affection. Carlos' "Bildung" is not a learning from "life" alone, as with Tasso and the Prince of Homburg where there is little more than a basic tragic, but edifying configuration of hero and environment; Carlos learns from calculated efforts by those around him to improve him. Schiller's hero, more than either Goethe's or Kleist's, *must* be educated; his "Bildungsprozeß" is a foregone conclusion when the play begins.

In this same context it should be added that there is an important difference between Carlos' development and that of Tasso and the Prince of Homburg from the standpoint of the "other world." Carlos is faced with two antagonists, Philipp, who is responsible for his fall, and Posa, who is responsible for his insight. Carlos and Posa stand together against the larger antagonist of Philipp's court and, at least for Posa, there is never a serious thought of accommodation to the other side. Philipp's world is, in a Storm and Stress sense, still too wrong to permit accommodation, and Posa's ideal of freedom too uncompromising. Carlos' "Bildungsprozeß" is not an effort toward adjustment to the main antagonist, Philipp, but it is a reawakening of his noble spirit which has been suppressed by his passion for Elisabeth. In this effort, Posa is his antagonist, and in the end it is Posa whom Carlos approaches and Posa who brings about his insight. Accommodation takes place between Carlos and Posa, and then the two still stand united in their political thinking against Philipp. This antagonist relationship is very different from that in TASSO and the PRINCE OF HOMBURG, where the court and personal antagonist are one and the same, and where "Bildung" is a movement toward accommodation with an opposite world. In TASSO and the PRINCE the antagonist structure is dualistic too, i.e. Tasso against Antonio and the court, the Prince against the law and the Elector, but here the "other world" causes both fall and insight. Because Carlos' learning process involves no accommodation with the main antagonist, but is limited to a personal rehabilitation which serves only to strengthen the gap between the two worlds, Schiller's play stands closer to the Storm and Stress plays than our other two dramas.

In DON CARLOS, as in all of Schiller's plays, is reflected Schiller's lifelong struggle with the problem of human freedom. The Wars of National Liberation in the Netherlands are used as Schiller's vehicle to symbolize this larger human problem. Since his days in the Karlsschule when Schiller had experienced almost total lack of freedom for his own person, Schiller was intent on defining the limits of personal freedom possible to man. All of Schiller's dramas center on this problem, and in the early plays it reveals itself as an open clash between youthful idealism and established, mostly despotic, power. Only in DON CARLOS does this political tendency take the form of an organized political program. Schiller wrote the play during the years between the American and the French Revolutions, a time when the idea of freedom was on everyone's lips. In the summer of 1786, when the Posa-scene was written, this idea had reached its height in the Körner-circle, which formed Schiller's milieu at the time, and where politics, especially politics in the humanistic sense, was always a major topic of conversation. Schiller recalls in the BRIEFE ÜBER DON CARLOS one of these conversations, albeit fictitious, which supposedly formed the basis for the CARLOS-drama:

> Rufen Sie sich, lieber Freund, eine gewisse Unterredung zurück, die über einen Lieblingsgegenstand unsers Jahrzehnts — über Verbreitung reinerer, sanfterer Humanität, über die höchstmögliche Freiheit der INDIVIDUEN bei des Staats höchster Blüte, kurz, über den vollendetsten Zustand der Menschheit, wie er in ihrer Natur und ihren Kräften als erreichbar angegeben liegt — unter uns lebhaft wurde und unsre Phantasie in einen der lieblichsten Träume entzückte, in denen das Herz so angenehm schwelgt.[2]

VERBREITUNG REINERER, SANFTERER HUMANITÄT — such is the theme of DON CARLOS as defined by Schiller. Neither love nor friendship, but the hope to create a new world ("Das kühne Traumbild eines neuen Staates,/Der Freundschaft göttliche Geburt" (4280—81)) forms, according to Schiller, the unifying theme of his "Freiheitsdrama." Coupled with the political motif is Schiller's belief in the individual's ability to do the noble, i.e. in a struggle between inclination and duty to choose the virtuous path. The figure of Carlos is Schiller's embodiment of this idea, and first the joining of this idea to the political theme makes the drama complete:

> Unter beiden Freunden bildet sich ... ein ENTHUSIASTISCHER ENTWURF, DEN GLÜCKLICHSTEN ZUSTAND HERVORZUBRIN-GEN, DER DER MENSCHLICHEN GESELLSCHAFT ERREICHBAR IST, UND VON DIESEM ENTHUSIASTISCHEN ENTWURFE, WIE ER NÄMLICH IN KONFLIKT MIT DER LEIDENSCHAFT ERSCHEINT, handelt das gegenwärtige Drama.[3]

Ultimately it is Carlos who also saves the political idea from tarnish. For while Posa derogates from his noble intentions by his sudden excess of hubris, Carlos redeems his friend's improvident action by his final avowal of loyalty to the now once again common goal. In this way too, Carlos is the real hero of Schiller's play. As E. L. Stahl writes: "Except for the prince, the drama does not end on a note of moral triumph. Schiller shows how passion is conquered by idealism in Don Carlos: he also shows how idealism is defeated by its own extremes in Posa.[4]

[2] Achter Brief.
[3] *Ibid.,* achter Brief.
[4] *Friedrich Schiller's Drama. Theory and Practice* (Oxford, 1954), p. 40.

Goethe, in a conversation with Caroline Herder,[5] defined the theme of TASSO, its "eigentlichen Sinn," as the "Disproportion des Talents mit dem Leben." Tasso is not a man of feeling as such, he is a *poet.* Tasso's creative talent forms the heart of his being; it is his "raison d'être." Tasso, the person, is always concerned about his poetic work; his poetry, above all else, fills his mind from the beginning to the end of the play. In this sense Goethe's hero is not naive like our other young men. Tasso is fully accomplished in his art; in the realm of poetry he is completely mature. Tasso's "Bildung" is not necessary for the purpose of training him to his calling (he has already completed his greatest work when the play begins); neither is it a process by which Tasso leaves adolescence, as such, behind and enters manhood (one may assume, although it is not expressly stated, that Tasso is older in age than both Carlos and the Prince of Homburg). Tasso's "Bildung" proceeds, not out of youthful innocence *per se,* but out of his problem as a *poet,* out of his inability to accept his poetic existence with its inherent limitations. Tasso's "naiveté" exists only in relation to his artistic talent, in the purity of his expectations concerning his life as a poet in the social world. To quote Wolfdietrich Rasch:

> Es [Tasso's life] ist ein produktives Dasein, und die menschlichen Konflikte, in die es gerät, sind davon nicht abzulösen; sie entstehen nicht aus dem Missverhältnis der Innerlichkeit schlechthin mit der Welt, sondern aus der 'Disproportion des *Talents* mit dem Leben.[6]

Most older interpretations of Goethe's play fail to make this finer distinction that Tasso is first and foremost a poet and not just a young man. They see little more in Tasso than the customary individualist in conflict with objective reality, which, moreover, they usually regard as the "better" of the two sides. Only recently has the poet been given his due consideration. Not only Rasch, but also Elizabeth M. Wilkinson, for example, emphasizes the creative side of Tasso's personality as his eventual curse. Miss Wilkinson writes: "What makes Tasso Tasso as distinct from some creature of wayward moods and fancies is his creative power."[7] Also Benno von Wiese differentiates the aesthetic character of Goethe's hero: ". . . gerade darin liegt die ergreifend notwendige Aussage des TASSO, dass sie die dichterische Existenz als tragische Existenz begreift."[8]

In TASSO Goethe has painted a picture of the true artist and of his "Leiden am Leben" as a result of his creative talent. Tasso, for all his individuality, is more than just an eccentric paranoic poet; he embodies the classic qualities of

5  This conversation is recorded in a letter of March 20, 1789, from Caroline Herder to her husband.
6  Rasch, *op.cit.,* p. 19.
7  "Goethe's 'Tasso'. The Tragedy of a Creative Artist," *Publications of the English Goethe Society,* 15 (1945), p. 100.
8  *Die deutsche Tragödie von Lessing bis Hebbel* (Hamburg, 1961), p. 91.

the poet: increased sensitivity, vivid imagination, passionate feeling, a complete receptivity and oneness with Nature, a need for companionship and understanding but at the same time the desire to be alone, an intense drive towards art and the tendency to translate all experience into poetic form, a passion for work, etc. In the same way that Tasso represents the poet at all times and in all places, the court at Ferrara is symbolic for life as such, for the social structure in which the poet must live and with which he must come to terms. Ferrara is not chiefly a political entity like Philipp's court and the Brandenburg state; it is not the political power of his environment with which the young man is at odds. Neither is Ferrara primarily important for its similarity to the court culture of the 18th century or for its Renaissance background, but only as the social setting in which Tasso, the poet, lives and which forms the stage for his personal misfortune.

> Die Hofgesellschaft, die in Goethes Drama dargestellt ist, "meint" nicht einfach die reale höfische Gesellschaft der Zeit, auch nicht die der Renaissance, sondern sie steht ganz wesentlich für "Gesellschaft" überhaupt in ihrem Verhältnis zum Dichter. Sie ist, um als Symbol brauchbar zu sein, entzeitlicht.[9]

Tasso stands essentially alone and misunderstood in the world of practical purposes and definite goals as exemplified by Alfonso's court, and it is this fundamental "outsider" status which Tasso is unable to accept and which forms the basis for his downfall. The world of the court is governed by real considerations, political interests, a sense of utility, ambition and status. The poet is not essential to this world, his creativity is not necessary to Ferrara's existence, and as a result he feels that he is only an observer and not an integral part of it. This Tasso cannot accept. Unlike Goethe himself, Tasso is unable to live with the gap which must necessarily exist in some measure between the creative artist and the world of reality, and his attempts to overcome this gap inevitably lead to his downfall. Tasso wants to be a part of both worlds, he feels divided in his person, and he does not rest until his efforts to resolve his conflict lead to an irreversible offense against the existing social order, and banishment. In TASSO Goethe has demonstrated the tragic results of poetic genius when it fails to accept the limitations of its own existence, when it finds it impossible to adapt to the unavoidable distance between itself and the outside world. He has portrayed his mature knowledge that, if the poet cannot change his nature, if he cannot conform to reality, then he must at least learn to live with the schism which separates him from the world of practical affairs. "Für Goethe ist diese Art des Leidens mit dem Dichtertum selbst gesetzt, als seine notwendige

---

9  Rasch, *op.cit.*, p. 34.

Bedingung. Es ist dem Dichter auferlegt, jene "Doppelheit" zu bewältigen, den Zwiespalt auszuhalten."[10] Tasso's "Bildung" is the result of his failure to fulfill this basic requirement of his life. It is a more negative experience than either Carlos' or the Prince of Homburg's "Bildung" in the sense that it occurs only involuntarily and when there is no choice left. Tasso has no chance to rectify his failing; the most he can do is voice his understanding. Tasso's "Bildung" manifests itself only as a final tragic recognition of the reality of his situation. Nothing more positive comes of it than a last-minute, desparate, and outwardly imposed, insight into the full meaning of his calling as a poet.

TORQUATO TASSO is the first drama with the poet as dramatic hero. Goethe was the first author to make the poetic existence the main subject of a dramatic work. Goethe had depicted the poet earlier himself, for example in WILHELM MEISTERS THEATRALISCHE SENDUNG and in the poem ZUEIGNUNG (1784), but Tasso is the first poet to be put on the stage. Goethe did not have an easy job to portray the poet dramatically, a person whose deeds exist not in visible activity, but in words and moreover usually in solitude. The poet is not the most likely figure for a stagework. And yet Goethe was immensely successful. Miss Wilkinson, in her very perceptive essay quoted above, has shown how Goethe does not ask us to accept Tasso's talent merely on hearsay, but how on various occasions he actually shows the poet in the act of creation on the stage. Goethe's play has served as model for countless literary works dealing with the creative artist throughout the 19th and 20th centuries, from Hölderlin's EMPEDOKLES to Hermann Broch's TOD DES VERGIL, but according to Emil Staiger at least, Goethe's TASSO has never been surpassed in its depth of insight into the nature of the poet:

> Er [Tasso] ist ein Dichter und nichts als dies, als solcher aber in den Bedingungen seines Schaffens, in dem Geheimnis seiner Begabung, in seinem Ruhm und seiner Not so ganz durchschaut, dass keine Dichter-psychologie der nächsten Jahrzehnte und unseres Jahrhunderts das Urbild auch nur annähernd erreicht.[11]

In the span of twenty years between the creation of Goethe's TASSO and Kleist's PRINZ FRIEDRICH VON HOMBURG the world saw a decline of the court culture immortalized in Goethe's play and the rise of the state as the social context in which the individual reached maturity. Revolutions on two continents and the Napoleonic Wars with their aftermath throughout Europe led to the dissolution of the Ancien Régime and to the birth of Nationalism, which was to become the predominant philosophical basis of government to the present day. The rise of Nationalism accounts for the main difference in social

---

10 *Ibid.,* p. 61.
11 *Goethe,* Vol. 1 (Zürich, 1952), p. 393.

setting between Kleist's play and its predecessors. The Prince's reality is the Prussian state, with its military codes of honor and justice, its patriotic fervor, and its unswerving respect for discipline, law, and order. The condition for "Bildung" in Kleist's PRINZ FRIEDRICH VON HOMBURG is the romantic individualist in conflict with the objective realm of the nationalist state.

Kleist's last play is a product of Kleist's turn to patriotism as a last effort to find meaning in his life. Kleist's whole life had been a struggle with the state, earlier as a rejection of it for the call to be a poet, and later, when the Napoleonic incursions had left the once proud and self-reliant Prussia a humiliated and occupied country, as a passionate expression of loyalty and devotion. Kleist returned to the state with the same dedication that he evinced for every undertaking of his life. The state became for him in his final years a last hope to find a reason to live after his repeated failures to find an anchor in his writings, to acquire the fame that he had set himself as his life's goal. Kleist vowed to awaken his countrymen to the salvation of Germany from foreign subjection. The German states as a whole, as a "fatherland," not just Prussia alone, became important to Kleist. Kleist now viewed the relationship of the individual to his country as an inviolable bond, as a "Du-relationship" so often associated with Kleist's name, and therefore the French influence and threat to German independence was unbearable to him. Kleist manifested his patriotic zeal outwardly by writing two additional plays as well as a number of tendentious poems. The tenor of the plays is a reversal from the one-time supremacy of the individual over outer threats to his freedom, to a subordination of the individual to the prevailing social order. The HERMANNS-SCHLACHT is the only outrageously partisan play that Kleist produced, and in this work the state is presented as absolutely right against the claims of the individual. In the PRINCE OF HOMBURG this duality balances out again.

Kleist's last play is a masterpiece of opaque purpose. The conflict here is presented with such dramatic skillfulness that it is almost impossible to say whether Kleist is advocating the state's cause to the claims of the Prince or the Prince's cause to the claims of the state. Both possibilities have been defended by critics in great detail, but there is still no conclusive answer and there probably never will be because Kleist left no personal testimony concerning his intentions in this, his most perfect, play. In the end, the most thorough critics are left to speculate on the basis of Kleist's known political leanings at the time when the PRINCE was written, and to draw their conclusions from the apparent outline of the play's events, taking also into consideration of course their knowledge of Kleist's poetic tendencies. Viewed from all of these angles, the PRINCE is as much a "Bildungsdrama" as CARLOS and TASSO. This is not to say that Kleist unquestionably supports the state over its young prince; Kleist's drama is not a glorification of the Prussian spirit. The problem here is presented with equal fairness to both sides, but with the outcome that the Prince yields ultimately to a higher reality. In the collision between youthful autism and established authority in Kleist's PRINCE OF HOMBURG, the individual gives way to the community, the community does not change to meet the wishes of the individual. The community remains essentially stationary; the individual submits, at least on the surface, to its fixed patterns. Now, whether or not Kleist is saying that the community in this case is "right," is beside the point; the fact is that from the standpoint of "Bildung," the Prince is the one who is educated to the ways of the community.

The conflict in the PRINCE OF HOMBURG develops between two main characters, the Prince, a young leader of the Prussian cavalry, and the Elector, who represents the corporate ideals of the Prussian state. The Prince, a victim of his dreamy nature and of a chain of unusual events, violates a rule of military warfare and is condemned to death. His final insight comes when the Elector makes him responsible for his own fate by placing that decision into his own hands. This causes a change in attitude from abject terror at the thought of death to an affirmation of the state's decision that he should die. Whatever the inner motive, the Prince forfeits at the Elector's stimulus his own claims to life to accept the verdict of the law of the state.

As was pointed out in the last chapter, the Prince is the first of Kleist's characters to reach a reconciliation with the outside world. The PRINCE OF HOMBURG is the single one of Kleist's plays in which external reality is materialized; up to then it was always simply a vague force against which the hero collided. Now the outside world assumes real features in the form of the Prussian state, and not only is this reality "real," but now it is also no longer evil. The antagonist has a righteousness of his own. The struggle in the PRINCE unfolds between two equally valid forces, though these are not equally matched. Both sides have claims to be considered, and it is these claims which are unevenly weighted. The establishment, with age and tradition on its side, has the preponderant advantage when a threat to its dominian occurs.

Because we are so often grouping CARLOS, TASSO, and the PRINCE OF HOMBURG together for the purpose of exploring our theme of "Bildung," it has been necessary to also point out the historical and thematic differences in the plays. In CARLOS a political message dominates. Carlos must be re-oriented to Posa's ideals of freedom, and to this end he must conquer his love for Elisabeth. TASSO'S problem is not political, but deeply personal. Ferrara is not mainly a political entity and not philosophically intolerable. What Goethe is showing is the timeless struggle of the artist in adjusting to the other world and that this adjustment is necessary. The PRINCE OF HOMBURG belongs to a later age historically and reflects the political rise of Brandenburg and the post-Napoleonic rise in nationalism. The Prince, like Tasso, is a victim of his own character. He is the romanticist individual pitted against the legalistic state, and he must conform.

Chapter 4:
## PRECONDITIONS FOR "BILDUNG"

Three young men, all naive and idealistic, all dreaming about goals of love and fame, all "men of feeling," pure, humanistically inclined, believing in a life's calling and the right to pursue that calling; three court environments, each proven and established, each worldly, unromantic, concerned mainly about preserving the status quo: thus the stage is set for the dramatic conflicts which follow in the plays DON CARLOS, TORQUATO TASSO and PRINZ FRIEDRICH VON HOMBURG. The dramatic situation which promotes the likelihood for "Bildung" in each of our works is one that pits the unspoiled and idealistic young man against an established and realistic court. The court not only sets the social stage for all of the action that takes place, but it also functions as a political entity, a role which it asserts more or less (TASSO less) aggressively in each play. Some of the young man's differences with the court are on these grounds of law and government, and these differences are exacerbated as the personal problems intensify. The young man stands essentially apart from his environment, concerned with personal goals of happiness and success, and frustrated by the court for whose peculiar problems he lacks affinity and understanding. The court, standing directly in the young man's way, is in each case conservative, bound by law and tradition, and has commitments and objectives that the hero instinctively cannot accept (the Prince of Homburg rejects them involuntarily). The sides are not equally divided in this struggle, for the court has all of the established power, including that of the Church in CARLOS and TASSO, on its side. It is older and more sophisticated than its young citizens, and it must of necessity protect its own interests against the ambitions of a single individual. Quite naturally then, the court becomes an obstacle for the young man as he probes into his life and tries to find his particular place in society in his own way. He is soon in deep conflict with the mores of the generations before him, and the court looms up for him as a large impersonal antagonist that he is crashing into headlong.

There is an obvious universality about this "young man versus the establishment" theme, and although, as has been elaborated in the foregoing chapter, the circumstances in these plays are highly individualized (himanitarian crown prince against a despotic empire, poet versus society, dreamy unorthodox prince in a Prussian setting), one has the feeling that Carlos, Tasso, or the Prince of Homburg might be any young man standing at the threshold of life, and that Philipp's court, Ferrara, and the Brandenburg state represent the world in general in which all youth must learn to live.

Just what is it that these young men want from life? What are their goals and how legitimate are these goals? Broadly stated, they want two things: (1) love, fame, acceptance — the selfish things, and (2) a better world in which to live, a chance to proceed with their calling with some degree of personal freedom and "Humanität." Of these wants, the most significant one for the learning process is the desire for acceptance. These young men are not rebels, engaged in open rebellion against society above all else. They are not typical Storm and Stress heroes, champions of freedom like Posa, or persons who insist on living to their own liking at anyone's expense. These heroes all have a high station in life and a calling of an aristocratic nature which they accept in principle. Although there is much "Storm and Stress" in each of them, these young men all want to fit into their environment and to contribute positively to its welfare. Even Carlos, who stands farthest away from his environmental focus, seeks a personal bond with his father and is initially willing to perform his duties as crown prince; his susceptibility to Posa, whom he actually approaches, is of course clear. And Tasso, who has often been misinterpreted as a rampant egotist, states clearly at one point that freedom will never rule his soul (928–32). All of these young men feel a distinct need to be loved and respected by their social circle, and this desire for acceptance gives them some feeling of relationship to society, which in turn provides the basis upon which "Bildung" or an adjustment to society ultimately takes place. This need for approval also creates the impetus for each hero's undoing, because it is partly his efforts to become a part of the other world which lead to the collision. The court will not, and indeed, cannot, accommodate to the hero's wishes as they exist, and the hero falls.

The young man's problem with the court, then, is not that he wants to escape it or overthrow it, but that he is seeking something beyond its conferable limits. These goals interfere with the court's established order, and they also cloud the hero's true calling. The idea of "calling" plays an important part in each hero's maturation process. Initially, there is a discrepancy between the hero's true calling and what he considers to be his calling. All of these young men are caught at the beginning in a web of illusion; they live essentially apart from reality and are absorbed in private dreams. Like most young people, they are occupied primarily with themselves and their own happiness, and have not yet faced the reality of their situation. The world, which is still opening itself up to them, appears still to hold promise for each of their fondest desires. Even Carlos, who has learned most about his "reality" when the play begins, still nurtures hopes for a future with Elisabeth. All of these young men have yet to be initiated into the true meaning of their lives, and one result of their confrontation with the court is that they are brought to this point.

Of the three heroes, Carlos needs "Bildung" in the sense of calling, of maturing to his responsibilities, most. He is professionally, and also as a person, the most immature of the three. His experiences prepare him, not for his legal calling as successor to Philipp, but for his nobler calling as Posa's emissary and alter ego.

When the play opens, Carlos has already been confronted with his world. It is immediately clear that Don Carlos must be rehabilitated. He comes on the stage in a "fallen" state, and the reasons for his condition are carefully made clear through references to his past. This first fall is not a minor experience for Carlos. It has two main causes and it has consequences which set up the political thread of the plot, which then runs through to the end. The first cause for Carlos' initial fall is his love for Elisabeth, the queen, his father's wife. We learn that Carlos had legitimate opportunity to fall in love with her and that, after that had happened, he came home to find his father married to her. Even before this, his relationship to his father had never been intimate or mutually satisfying. The second reason for Carlos' depressed and erratic behavior, as the play opens, is that he is completely idle within the bounds of this antagonistic court. He sees but cannot realize his love; the court personnel are scheming against him and his father does not trust him with a proper assignment or send him away. The consequences of all this are that Carlos has lost his humanistic enthusiasm to build a new world with Posa, and this sets the stage for Posa to appear and to redefine Carlos' mission in life for him and to rehabilitate him.

Posa's reason for returning to Madrid is to solicit Carlos' assistance in executing a plan that he has devised for the liberation of the Netherlands, a plan which envisions Carlos in the leading role. His grave disappointment at finding Carlos in his fallen state is thus very understandable:

> So war es nicht, wie ich Don Philipps Sohn
> Erwartete.                                    (148–49)
>                     Das ist
> Der löwenkühne Jüngling nicht, zu dem
> Ein unterdrücktes Heldenvolk micht sendet –   (152–54)

Posa has only one thought on meeting Carlos: he must somehow reawaken in his friend his former interest for the political ideals. That Carlos is amenable to Posa's henceforth manipulation of him forms the subsequent current for Carlos' final insight.

Carlos is agreeable to Posa's and/or Elisabeth's plans for several reasons. First of all, he has a major need for the affection of those he loves. More important to him than the fulfillment of his own wishes as they exist, is the compliance to the wishes of others in order to assure himself of their attachment. Thus when Elisabeth agrees to help Posa by inspiring Carlos to renounce his love for a higher cause, Carlos responds willingly. He wants to please Elisabeth to be certain of her further devotion. Also, Carlos is miserable and wants to find a way out of his suffering, and this is an opportunity to escape both his surroundings and his passion. He knows the risks he takes both for himself and for Elisabeth if he stays at court, and his basically noble nature causes him to have pangs of conscience on moral grounds. In spite of the grave injustices that Carlos has suffered at the hands of his father, he shows the stature of his character in the fact that he still respects Philipp's legal rights to Elisabeth and does not hate him. Schiller himself says that all the essential qualities for greatness lie in Carlos and that they must simply be rendered unassailable by this final trial. According to Schiller, as soon as Carlos will have conquered this last weakness, he will be ready to be king:

> Der Jüngling nämlich, zu dem wir uns dieser ausserordentlichen Wirkung versehen sollen, musste zuvor Begierden übermeistert haben, die einem solchen Unternehmen gefährlich werden können; gleich jenem Römer musste er seine Hand über Flammen halten, um uns zu überführen, dass er Manns genug sei, über den Schmerz zu siegen; er musste durch das Feuer einer fürchterlichen Prüfung gehen und in diesem Feuer sich bewähren .... Mit dieser Liebe allein hätte er es also zu tun, und *ganz* wird ihn die Tugend haben, wenn es ihm gelungen sein wird, auch noch diese Liebe zu besiegen.[1]

Carlos' immaturity lies mostly in his "Gefühlsmensch" nature, in his reactions from his heart instead of his mind. But just this shortcoming gives him potential for growth. His openness and tendency to react spontaneously, especially to those he loves, are precisely the qualities that enable him to respond to Posa's and Elisabeth's manipulation. Thus Carlos' lack of sophistication has its positive aspects as far as Posa's goal is concerned, and it is this naiveté which Posa exploits to his own ends.

With Elisabeth's help, Posa succeeds in rekindling Carlos' political interests to the point where he is ready to try to persuade Philipp to send him as governor to the Netherlands instead of Alba. But this first effort by Posa only deepens Carlos' feelings toward Elisabeth by precipitating another illusion. This is actually Carlos' third state of illusion. He has already experienced two periods of illusion which are responsible for the fall he is in when the play opens. This third illusion precipitates the crash against Philipp which we see in the course of the dramatic action itself, and which entangles Carlos in the fateful triangle of court intrigue which then, with the interaction of Posa, promotes his insight in the manner that Schiller envisions it. Carlos, caught up in his eagerness to please his mentors, and confident of success with his father, approaches Philipp openly and naively, according to character, and must then pay the consequences of his personally good, but highly unrealistic, intentions.

The usual misunderstandings that exist between the creative artist and society in general lie at the heart of the problems that Tasso, the poet, faces in the world of Ferrara. Both sides have claims to be respected. The difficulty arises from the fact that neither side is willing to accept the other side as it is, but insists on

---

[1] BRIEFE ÜBER DON CARLOS, neunter Brief.

making its own demands upon it. The court wants to change Tasso and Tasso wants the court to accommodate fully to his presence. Both parties want and need the other for their existing way of life — the problem is not that they are rejecting each other; but they want each other on their own terms and without acknowledging the basic and unalterable differences between them.

Ferrara is a world of polite form and decorum. Tasso, the unpredictable and unconforming poet, causes by his very presence a disharmony in these surroundings. The mere fact that an exceptional person lives in Ferrara's gentle circle creates friction. The court is aware that Tasso is "different" and that he must to a certain extent be tolerated, but at the same time it cannot help wishing that Tasso were more like itself, and his presence is a constant source of irritation to its members. Thus the many conversations about "changing" Tasso. From the moment the action begins, all talk touches in some way, usually centers around, the poet and his dissimilarity to the world about him. Everyone has his own ideas about what is wrong with Tasso, about why he does not "fit in," and what is needed to improve him. From this standpoint alone, the drama is a "Bildungsdrama." From the court's point of view, the theme of the play is, or at least *should* be, the education of the poet to its own mode of life. Duke Alfonso is patronizing towards Tasso, he wants the poet present to enhance the court's prestige and he watches over him like a fine possession, but basically he cannot understand the poet's nature and cannot summon up any real affection for him. The man of public life tends to view the poet more as an asset for his own esteem than as an individual with private needs and rights, and with a worthiness of his own. While it is true that the Duke means well by Tasso — it was he who first gave the poet the leisure to develop his talent by freeing him from the want of his unhappy childhood — now that he has Tasso at court, he is, in spite of himself, dissatisfied with the poet's conduct and seeks to reform him to meet the court's standards. Tasso, acutely sensitive to his environment and in critical need of the court's recognition and approval, feels this lack of sympathy and suffers from it. Tasso has an identity problem which stems from his uncertainty about his own existence as a poet. Tasso knows that he does not accord with the other world, that, in comparison to the visible activity which occupies Ferrara, his work is questionably useful, and Tasso cannot reconcile himself to the division which separates him from the world of reality. Tasso suffers from what he defines as a tendency to "dissolve" in the face of the tangible contributions of the people around him (797—800). Without sacrificing any of his own identity, Tasso wants to be a full-fledged member of the society in which he lives. Just as the court covets Tasso for selfish purpose, Tasso needs Ferrara for several reasons. First of all, Tasso is dependent on the court's patronage for his physical existence. As a poet in the Renaissance world, Tasso needs the protection of a prince in order to have the necessary freedom to write. Secondly, it is only in such a courtly atmosphere that poetry is promoted. Only here does a practical appreciation of the arts exist. And finally, Tasso must refer to court life for the knowledge of the world which he needs for his poetry. Here, in the world of affairs, is where Tasso gets the material that he casts into poetic form. Tasso needs the court for all of these reasons, and he is grateful to the Duke for his support (417f.), but yet he is not willing to accept the court's codes of conduct which exclude him from full membership in its ranks. This is not to say that Tasso wants to force himself upon the court; on the contrary, he does his best to stay within acceptable limits of behavior. It means that when the poet feels a threat to his own identity, when he feels denied complete approbation by the court, he reacts defensively, not out of a deliberate wish to dishonor the court, but out of a basic insecurity which he is unable to conquer. And these reactions, provoked as they are by a protective instinct just as uncontrollable on the side of the court, serve then to enmesh the poet in an inescapable net of destruction.

The laureation scene, which is the starting-point for all of Tasso's troubles and which gives rise to that illusion in Tasso which makes the coming collision all the more shattering, points up the difference in the two worlds very well. Right here, in the attitudes of the two sides towards this event, can be seen the gap which exists between the world of the poet and the world around him. Wolfdietrich Rasch calls the laurel wreath symbolic for Tasso's whole conflict with the court.[2] For the court, the crowning of the poet is a moment of fitting distinction for an artist whom it calls its own and who has just completed his greatest work of art. The court does not mean to take the occasion lightly, it truly wishes to honor Tasso and to express its appreciation and pride in him, but it fails to understand the great significance which this act of laureation has for Tasso. The court, bound up in its material view of life, cannot identify with a purely symbolic act. For Tasso, on the other hand, this scene represents a climax in his life. It is a moment of extreme sensitivity, a moment filled with both joy and pain. At once his whole poet's existence is confirmed and his world of art is placed on an equal level beside the world of the state. Tasso's elaborate reaction to this celebration of his talent is caused by the poet's vivid awareness of the age-old glory attached to the laurel. Tasso is at pains to conceal the ecstatic feeling, and at the same time the fear of unworthiness, which he feels in his heart. This moment bears, besides these conflicting emotions, much more subtle significance for the poet,[3] but the important point here is that with this event Tasso thinks that the gap between himself and Ferrara has been resolved and that the court now accepts him with full respect. For the time being, in this climax to his artistic efforts, Tasso's conflict is lifted and his search for identity ended. Tasso rejoices in the illusion that his poet's world has been granted

---

2   Rasch, *op.cit.,* p. 107.
3   Compare: Rasch, *ibid.,* p. 104f.

complete endorsement by his associates. This illusionary condition is then staggered to dangerous proportions in the following act when the Princess disguisedly, but nonetheless unmistakably, confesses her love for the poet. Misled by her subconscious need to assure herself of the poet's love, the Princess, who shares the closest natural bond with Tasso and wants least of all to harm him, unwittingly adds to the poet's confusion by instilling hopes in him for a possible future together. Both, Tasso and the Prince of Homburg, fall victim to a double illusion which increases their vulnerable states and makes their subsequent falls doubly devastating. In both cases, a confession of love follows an apparent achievement of fame. Tasso now, with good reason, expects full recognition form the outside world, and when this world, embodied in Antonio, fails to give it, the poet falls.

Antonio's return at the very moment of Tasso's laureation forms the other half of the preparatory setting for Tasso's undoing. Antonio enters the scene at the same moment that the poet reaches his zenith, and takes offense at the decoration adorning Tasso's head. Antonio, a statesman who considers his own occupation more deserving of distinction than the less demonstrable, and for Antonio merely entertaining, accomplishments of his rival beneficiary, cannot conceal his annoyance and is provoked to ill-humor by the whole event. His first words to Tasso bode ill for the future:

> Du wirst mich wahrhaft finden, wenn du je
> Aus deiner Welt in meine schauen magst. (583—84)

The reader immediately feels a disparaging distinction between the world of the poet and Antonio's world. Nor is this a fleeting mood with Antonio. He remains in this state until Tasso, prodded by the Princess, approaches him to seek his friendship, at which time Tasso's illusion is rudely and quickly dispersed.

The Prince of Homburg has no conscious dispute either with himself or with his environment. As a typically Kleistian character, the Prince is completely at one with himself and his world when the play begins. The Prince enjoys the most love and acceptance of the three heroes from his court surroundings, he is aware of no breach between himself and his inherited calling, and although he has failed twice to win victory for the Elector in battle, the royal family cherishes him as its own son and natural successor. He is for the Elector and for the other officers their, if prodigal, still most beloved, warrior. There is no inevitable reason for what happens to the Prince; he is not doomed in advance by a necessarily tragic constellation of hero and environment. Although the Prince is atypical as a Prussian officer, as the opening scene confirms, the tragic make-up of the Prince's milieu arises suddenly and unexpectedly in a one-time, and fateful, meeting of events. The Prince's only initial problem is that he has a tendency to dwell within himself, to wander into personal dreams at inopportune times. This subjective quality was probably the reason for his previous double blunder on the battlefield, and it is also that flaw which leads to his vulnerability as the play begins. The Prince is inclined to live mentally apart from his surroundings, to reside in a personal reality divorced from the reality outside, not from a conscious effort to escape his world, but from an involuntary leaning towards introversion. The Prince likes what he is, he is at peace with his profession and dedicated to the Elector whom he loves and admires, but he simply has not yet faced up to the full responsibility of his calling. He has never considered the full import of his actions or reached a firm relationship with the Brandenburg code, and his "Bildung" turns out to be an inordinately harsh test of his fitness to be a Prussian officer.

In each of our three dramas, the dissonance between the young man and his environment is impressed upon the reader in an exposition which warns of a coming collision. In CARLOS the portentous nature of the approaching interview with Philipp is conveyed to the audience when Carlos tells of his love for Elisabeth and emphasizes the incompatibility between himself and his father. In TASSO the whole first act with the laureation and the accompanying dialogues, plus Antonio's untimely entrance, serve to illuminate the rift between the poet and Ferrara. The variance of the Prince of Homburg to his surroundings is graphically pointed up in the garden scene when the Prince is caught sleepwalking in the advent of battle. A noble young man, half dressed, at midnight, absentmindedly winding himself a laurel wreath in the light of the moon, is hardly the familiar image of a Prussian officer! This "Unart des Geistes" (39) seduces the Elector to indulge in a little game with the Prince which generates a whole series of complications and envelops the Prince in an impenetrable sea of enchantment. The Elector, wishing to test the strength of the Prince's somnambulist state, takes the wreath from the Prince's hand, winds his own medaillion around it and hands it to Natalie who prepares to place it on the Prince's head. The action is not realized, however, because at this moment the Elector withdraws with Natalie, surprised and frightened back by a sudden movement of the Prince who stands up in an unexpected gesture of agreement. Apparently, all this fits right in with the Prince's dream. On retreating, Natalie leaves behind a glove which Homburg inadvertently brushes from her hand. This glove, which the Prince discovers on awakening, becomes the catalyst for the Prince's whole subsequent involvement. Later that night, while taking down battle orders for the following morning, the Prince discovers that the glove belongs to Natalie, and suddenly the Prince's dream assumes real proportions. The glove, which belongs to both worlds, is for the Prince a pledge from reality that his dream will soon be realized, i.e. that he will be victorious in battle tomorrow, thus earning the Elector's favor, and that Natalie's love will also then be his. The dream is a prophetic vision of things to come. It is unclear whether

Homburg's love for Natalie was previously a conscious part of the Prince's life or whether it is first perceived by this event; what is clear is that from this moment on the Prince has only one goal, to follow his new "calling" unimpeded.

All of our heroes are men of feeling in one sense. They all react emotionally rather than deliberately. The Prince's "feeling" is different from that of his Storm and Stress-related predecessors, however. "Feeling" is not important to the Prince primarily as a human right, as a legitimate code of existence to be defended against conventional form. The Prince's "Gefühl" is synonymous with his very being. Like most of Kleist's characters, the Prince lives his feeling as an unconscious shadowy presentiment of what he must do, of how he must act. The Prince does not *know* what his new "calling" is, he merely senses it, senses it with all certainty, and pursues it with like unconditionality. As Elsbeth Leber defines it: "... [das Kleistische] Gefühl ist die unbewusste Gewissheit der eigenen Bestimmung."[4] While Carlos and Tasso pursue their goals consciously, the Prince follows his calling unconsciously and involuntarily. His insight results in the same manner. The Prince never questions, never thinks, only reacts, reacts in accordance with an indisputable inner voice at the heart of his being with no other considerations involved.

Thus it is that the Prince becomes entwined in the seemingly magical web which leads to his undoing. Having failed in his trancelike state to hear the proper instructions, he enters the battle prematurely, violating a precise order and forcing the Elector to call for his arrest. But this arrest comes only much later, and in the meantime the Prince's dream is even more exaggerated by victory on the battlefield, by Natalie's actual confession of love following the victory, and by her willingness to accept him as a protector to replace the Elector, reportedly killed in battle. This completes the Prince's state of euphoria and he is ready for the approaching debacle.

We have seen how, in all three plays, the hero naturally stands apart from his world, and how this situation is exaggerated by the creation of an illusionary state in the hero as part of the exposition. The preconditions for "Bildung" are unique in each play but yet they are alike in that they all culminate on a similar plateau of illusion from which the hero's fall then occurs.

---

[4] *Das Bild des Menschen in Schillers und Kleists Dramen* (Bern, 1969), p. 151.

## Chapter 5:
## THE "BILDUNGSPROZESS"

### *From Illusion to Fall: The Question of Guilt*

The three heroes, Carlos, Tasso, and the Prince of Homburg, in their illusionary states, pursue their goals directly and absolutely. Spurred on by hopes of love, fame, and conquest, the young men at these moments are filled with a new and driving confidence in themselves. They want to test themselves in their own eyes and prove themselves to the women they love, and their natural tendency to act is provoked to the bursting point. This leads them to a collision with reality, and it is this collision with its consequences that forms the subject of this chapter.

The question of guilt in any drama of merit is a complex one. This is true for all of our dramas, where the guilt is distributed among many factors. In none of the three plays does the blame for the hero's downfall rest with one party alone, but both the young man and his environment share the responsibility. Guilt is distributed, if not evenly, at least intentionally between both sides. In using the term "guilt" with reference to the court environment, we do not judge the moral or political rightness or wrongness of the court, we do not question the laws or customs that exist, we simply accept the environment as an existing fact with which the hero must come to terms in his struggle for identity. The *hero's* fate is the point of issue in each play, there is never a serious question that the surrounding world could change to accommodate to the young man.

Initially, the young men are guilty only of their youth and immaturity. With the possible exception of Carlos, none of the three heroes commits an intentional offense against his society; none is trying in his illusion to overthrow the establishment or to revolutionize an accepted form of behavior.[1] The heroes succumb involuntarily to a blindness which causes them to misinterpret reality. Here, the fallibility of human action so peculiar to drama is nicely demonstrated, in that, as soon as the heroes undertake an action to realize their goals, they fall. They become involved in a situation which does not enhance their personal freedom, as hoped, but takes away from it. Coincidentally, this loss of freedom continues up to the time of each hero's arrest and imprisonment, where it is total.

---

[1] It has been indicated previously that Carlos differs at least from Posa in that he bears less responsibility for his actions. Carlos, in contrast to Posa, never considers the full weight of his request to his father, but acts from an emotional base, and the reaction is emotional in origin, not the result of a considered plan, when he beseeches Philipp for the Flanders assignment.

Yet, these young men cannot be exonerated from guilt for the initial event which precipitates their downfall. There is a certain culpability in the very immaturity of these dramatic figures. Each one has a constitutional inclination toward the impulsiveness which envelops him at the time of his illusion, and he has to be inherently guilty for the consequences. Friedrich Koch, in writing about the Prince of Homburg, takes exception to Gerhard Fricke's assertion that reality bears all of the blame for the Prince's calamity. Koch maintains that the Prince himself must be held responsible for his own fate because the Prince possesses the *tendency* to misinterpret reality, and this tendency is only brought to life by an unfortunate merging of reality with Homburg's inner consciousness. I agree. Not only in PRINZ FRIEDRICH VON HOMBURG but in all of our dramas, the young men, although guiltless as far as willful intent is concerned, still share an important part of the blame for the initial stages of their disasters.[2]

Each hero's share in the dramatic guilt is compounded when, in his trance-like state, he approaches reality in such a way that he presents a threat to society, against which society must then defend itself. Granted, that, idealistically, all three heroes have a certain right to their objectives and that, in a humanistic sense, their strivings are legitimate. Carlos and Posa certainly have a moral right to oppose Philipp's tyranny, and Carlos, historically, has legitimate claims to Elisabeth's love; Tasso, as concerns basic human drives, cannot be censured for his pure love for the Princess, neither can he be reproached for expecting more from his visit to Antonio; and the Prince of Homburg, to paraphrase numerous critics, is only dreaming about what ultimately becomes his anyway. Still, in the form that they envision the realization of their goals, the young men err against reality, and reality must counter the blow. The worlds of these heroes simply are not capable of bestowing such favors as the young men demand. They are in all instances severely structured worlds, worlds in which absolute striving is prohibited and where only limited freedom is allowed. Or, to state it another way, there is in each drama an unbridgeable gap between the ideal and the real, and the question of guilt in the hero is decided in the way he grapples with that reality.

Ultimately, the hero really offends his society to the degree that a question of law has to be invoked, and here is where his guilt is precisely pinpointed. The hero feels free to use the law to suit his own purpose in life, and he does this in a way which directly violates the prevailing statutes or deviates from accepted codes of conduct. Either he has never thought consciously about the law (Prince of Homburg), or the law for him is not an absolute (Tasso), or he is in plain disagreement with the law (Carlos). At this illusion-fall juncture of his life, each

---

[2] For Koch's discussion, see: Friedrich Koch, *Heinrich von Kleist. Bewusstsein und Wirklichkeit* (Stuttgart, 1958), p. 200f.

hero places himself above the law in some way, and that is how he initially falls into guilt. The world about him does not conduct itself according to whim and choice, but by the strict letter of rule and custom.

The whole play of DON CARLOS revolves around a struggle between the law of Philipp II's inquisitional Spain and the law as prompted by humanistic principles. Here, the young hero is still involved in a direct effort to change his society, and Carlos and Posa are ready to engage in open rebellion against Philipp's despotism. For Posa it is his obvious duty to fight Spanish rule, and Carlos, as his fledgling, follows Posa's directives. Carlos, in his interview with his father, stands in direct opposition to the political dictates of Philipp's kingdom. Philipp has good reason to mistrust his son and to deny his request because, although Carlos is not thinking directly about the consequences of his action, he is heading with this step onto a course which would soon lead to a showdown with his father's system of government. It is always an interesting question what Carlos would have done if Philipp had sent him as governor to the Netherlands. At this important moment, as his fate hangs in the balance, Carlos stands directly between Posa and Philipp in political thrust, and although he is not fully aware of his motives and is working from personal considerations, at some point, if his goal were realized, he would have to choose between loyalties, and at that point it is almost certain that he would follow Posa against his father. That point is never reached, but Carlos' failure to convince Philipp at this time, and his subsequent fall, are the result of a conflict of interpretation of the existing law and of a difference in approach to that law, which Philipp senses, although Carlos himself never faces the question squarely. In other words, Philipp has legitimate reason to reject Carlos, not only because Carlos may be in fact too young and inexperienced to assume such a role at this stage of his life, but also and more importantly for Philipp because an affirmative response to Carlos' plea would mean a serious threat to Philipp's further reign.

Tasso respects the law of Ferrara and is not working to subvert it, but he, too, looks to first principles and what the law *should* be. Tasso does not run into difficulty with the traditions of his society until he is irritated by Antonio to the point of drawing his sword in the pivotal scene between the two men. While it is clear that Tasso's whole presence at Ferrara and especially his love for the Princess are a constant pressure against the behavioral patterns of the court, Tasso himself does nothing overtly to displease his social circle until provoked by that circle. Only when Antonio incites Tasso by his mockery of the poet's laurel wreath following Tasso' solicitation of his friendship, does Tasso react in a manner contrary to the established decorum of Ferrara. Tasso is greatly forebearing in the face of Antonio's blatant insults. He tries very hard to avoid an open confrontation, but his honor is rightly offended by Antonio's unmistakable taunts, and the naive strain in the poet will not allow him to act for long in opposition to his real feeling or to assume an attitude which denies the true sense of the moment. Thus results his ultimate loss of composure and the drawing of swords.

The law for Tasso loses its meaning when it serves as a shield for such reprehensible behavior as Antonio permits himself in the duel scene. Tasso looks to the deeper meaning of the law than its mere outer dictates. What is ultimately right or wrong is decided for Tasso by inner feeling, and there is no question in his mind that Antonio is the real culprit at this meeting. Provocation to break the law is just as wrong in Tasso's, the fundamental poet's, estimation as an actual offense. That is why, although he is not thinking in such terms at the moment of contact, Tasso feels not only justified, but even called upon, to defend his honor when he repels Antonio — even at the risk of an open infringement of house rules. In Tasso's eyes his personal honor amounts to the honor of the entire court. Tasso fully expects the Duke's approbation of his conduct; thus his dismay, and even outright disbelief, when Alfonso censures him instead of Antonio. Tasso is at a loss to explain what, to his own way of thinking, should have been an obvious decision in his own favor. Tasso's fall is at bottom the result of two divergent approaches to life, one, that of the court, according to inherited form, the other, that of the naive poet, according to intrinsic human nature.

Tasso's love for the Princess and his ultimate infraction of Ferraran ethic are an extension of this gap in views concerning the existing law. The embrace scene with its devastating impact for the poet is of course more complex than a simple misinterpretation of permissible conduct. The embrace is the result of deeper psychological drives, but yet it, too, rests basically on a difference of approach to life by the lover and the environment which influences his beloved. In Renaissance society it was forbidden for the court poet to become emotionally involved with a member of the ruling family. As Wolfdietrich Rasch points out, it would have been more thinkable had Tasso carried on an actual affair with Leonore Sanvitale, a married woman, than to have a legitimate love relationship with the unmarried sister of the Duke.[3] Thus Tasso's love for the Princess is doomed from the beginning, and any move in the direction of its fulfillment leads lineally to disaster for the poet.

The Prince of Homburg, too, follows the voice of his heart when he violates the law on the battlefield. The Prince is somewhat different from his literary brothers, however, in that Kleist's hero has no conscious relationship to the law of his environs at the time of his fall. True, Friedrich von Homburg is a Prussian general and must therefore know Brandenburg law according to letter, and he himself attests that he knows it (486—87), but his own relationship to the military code of his society has not yet been tested when the drama unfolds, and

3  Rasch, op.cit., p. 147.

when he acts wrongly on the battlefield, he is following quite other drives that override any conditioning he may have had to the law. He is not thinking about the *law* at all — he has not even heard the orders of the day, but is under the power of involuntary forces which possess him completely for a while and which compel him to pursue victory in battle at all costs. Homburg, when he commits his fateful error, is reacting from a euphoric belief that fate has singled him out for personal glory. This belief is born from the extraordinary sequence of events that he experienced the night before, and has no basis in the reality of the present, a reality with a specific battle plan based on categorical military law. This is the reason that the Prince's fall is so much more severe than either Carlos' or Tasso's. For while all three heroes are unaware of their motives at the crucial moment, Carlos and Tasso at least know that their actions violate standard procedure. The Prince of Homburg, on the other hand, has not the slightest notion that he is doing anything wrong when he breaks the law. He honestly believes that his performance in battle is in complete accord with the demands of the moment and that he is serving the Elector just as faithfully on this day as on any other. Only later when he is arrested and reality begins to sink in, does the Prince think at all about his action in terms of the law, and then his lack of relationship to the law becomes clearly apparent. From the "Prussian" point of view, the Prince is deviant in his attitude that human feeling is more important than the strict letter of the law. Although Homburg's motives when he acted single-handedly in combat were not humanistically based, he expounds such principles now in protest to his arrest. Initially, he clings to the belief that the Elector, likewise, holds such views and that, as soon as the formal demands of the moment will have been met, he, too, will follow the voice of his heart and pardon the errant son. Until reality undeniably proves him wrong, the Prince refuses to accept the possibility that the Brandenburg state operates on any other basis, fundamentally, than compassion for human feeling first, law second. That he dwells so long in this belief shows to just what extent he is disoriented from a true concept of the prevailing law. Whether or not the Prince's basic relationship to the law ever changes, depends on how one interprets his final insight.[4]

From what has been said so far, one might get the impression that these heroes are champions of humanistic causes after all, at least against the backdrop of their not so human environments. Still, it must be remembered that these heroes are basically self-centered, and that when they fall, they fall as a result of pursuing personal, not philanthropic, goals. None of these protagonists is above all championing a cause outside of himself when he meets failure in his environment. Even Carlos wants mainly to satisfy his own needs with his visit to

---

[4] The Prince's insight, as well as the Elector's position, are subjects of later discussions.

Philipp. Only later, following the clash, does each hero's dissonance to his society become clear, either for the first time as in the Prince of Homburg's case, or as a repeated awareness with Carlos and Tasso, and then the hero voices humanistic principles as part of his protest. The efforts to instruct society are short-lived, however, and soon the young man falls back into himself and his own problems. In no case is the upsurge of humanity sustained, but it remains in each play a secondary issue in the *hero's* growth process. Until the final insight at least, humanistic endeavors do not play a protagonist-primary role in the young man's "Bildung," and then only for Carlos. Perhaps one reason why Carlos' final insight rings somewhat untrue is because selfless ideals remain to the end basically foreign to his nature. All three of our heroes are fundamentally "Gefühlsmenschen," reacting subjectively rather than for society-oriented, objective goals. They are more egoistic than altruistic. That is why, following their falls and their brief appeals to human understanding, they are soon caught up again within themselves and their own dilemmas. In each drama, the young man's effort to humanize his environment exists only as it is directly related to, and necessary for, his own peronal fate.

While it is true, then, that these protagonists are mostly victims at the onset of their falls, they all do, in the course of their undoing, become guilty of a real personal guilt. Each hero's fall takes place in more than one stage, and while initially the young man has not fallen within himself, he soon, as a result of the intervening events, suffers a lapse in behavior which brings a real personal guilt to him. In each play, this guilt is a moral failure which is basically foreign to the young man's nature, and which, when he recognizes it, produces in him a deep remorse, thus preparing him for the final insight and also constituting an important part of it. In Tasso's and the Prince of Homburg's cases, this low point immediately precedes the final insight, forming the culmination of their falls, and it is from this point that the heroes are ultimately raised. In Carlos' case, the moral low point (the intent to use the Eboli-letter as a means to win Elisabeth) has yet to be followed by a spiritual low resulting from Posa's supposed betrayal, but two points are important here: first, Carlos never sinks lower in behavior than at the end of the Eboli-scene and is already on the way towards regeneration following Posa's scolding; second, and more important to the idea of "Bildung," the personal guilt that Carlos recognizes and that directly paves the way for his final insight is his loss of trust in his friend, thus, as in the other works, a guilt bound up with a fall immediately preceding insight. Although the term "moral guilt" cannot be applied to Carlos' behavior at this time, it is important that, to Carlos' way of thinking, he has erred personally and seriously in his abandonment of faith in his friend, and that it is this error in combination with his whole love for Elisabeth, which always has a moral question in it for Carlos, that finally prepares him for insight.

All three heroes' personal failures are closely related to a loss of trust in the personal antagonist. The personal antagonist for these young men is an ambivalent figure. On the one hand, he is the person most responsible on the direct and immediate level for the hero's downfall. On the other hand, he is the person in each play who represents an attraction for the young man and whom the young man seeks to emulate in his developing life. Psychologically, each hero is dependent to a great degree on the recognition and approval of his adversary. For a time following the initial impact to fall, the young man strives to maintain trust in this person, or at least, in Tasso's case, he does not immediately abandon all judgment in his appraisal of Antonio. Finally, however, each hero's efforts to remain stable fail, and when this happens, he loses a hold on life such that he becomes vulnerable to a multitude of forces around him. Loss of trust in his mentor means that the young man loses touch with reality and falls open to the whim of the moment. For Carlos and the Prince of Homburg, imagined personal failure in their antagonists leaves the heroes in bleak despair. They find themselves facing a void as a result of their sudden spiritual aloneness, a field of dim prospects, at most, with which they cannot cope and which impels them to grasp onto the first entering thought as a means of support, as a way to escape the terrible reality of the moment. This attempt to achieve balance leads Carlos and the Prince to commit a second fateful act, this time to bring about the culmination of their falls. Just as impulsiveness in these young men, in Tasso too, initiated their downfalls, again it is a rash act, in all three cases, which preludes the climax of collapse. Carlos runs to Princess Eboli to beg permission to see Elisabeth, thus forcing Posa to take him prisoner, and the Prince of Homburg leaves his cell in a storm of passion to seek out the Electress, thus unwittingly taking himself past his gravesite and ushering in the fear-of-death scene.

Tasso's case is somewhat different from his companions in that Tasso is given to distrust as a constitutional flaw, and Antonio's rejection of him simply exaggerates this weakness in the poet to the point where it becomes critical. Tasso never had a personal trust-relationship with his antagonist, and his fall does not result from a loss of trust so much as from an unsuccessful effort to create such a bond between himself and the more experienced Antonio. When Antonio rejects Tasso's offer of friendship, it propels Tasso back into doubt about himself and his poet's work. He finds his poet's world placed once more in jeopardy by Antonio's refusal to accept him, and questions anew the validity of the artist's existence. External and unintended circumstances feed this situation to the climactic point where Tasso loses all touch with his surroundings, succumbs to an embrace of the Princess, and ends by blaspheming the entire court, thus pulling down a wall of moral guilt onto himself. It is from this level of blackest despair that, as in all three plays, insight occurs, and one finds himself asking, again as in all three plays, if perhaps the author's purpose in allowing the hero to sink so low is just for this reason, that only from such depths can insight follow. Or is it possibly in order to make the final insight all the more impressive?

The concepts of friendship and trust play an important part in the lives and works of each of our dramatic writers and in the literature of the Age of Goethe in general. It was in the eighteenth century that friendship first became a valid form of human expression. Up until that time, human emotions had by necessity been directed mostly towards God and the State, but during the Age of Enlightenment, as the Church and the State lost some of their traditional authority, the individual began to exercise more control over his own affairs, and personal bonds in private life assumed a position of greater importance. One could now express oneself in the private sphere, and have his feelings recognized.[5] The theme of friendship begins to fill German literature with Gellert and his followers, originating as part of the "Empfindsamkeits"-movement, and continues, increasing in intensity, through the period of Storm and Stress to the literature under discussion here. Our three dramas testify to a special kind of friendship which was born at this time and which reflects the "Bildungs"-idea of the Age of Goethe. A pedagogical friendship between a younger and an older man, such as that in real life between Goethe and Herder, forms one aspect of the protagonist-antagonist dramatic constellation in each of our plays, and the tension arising from this constellation, which has both its positive and negative sides, creates the impetus for each hero's downfall, and eventual enlightenment. The young man, in each case, both seeks, and at some point is cast out from, the favor of his personal antagonist, and a trust crisis in each drama forms the crux of the hero's downfall. A personal relationship based on absolute trust has an almost sacred quality in it for each of these young men. The Prince of Homburg is famous for his trust-relationship to the Elector and for the "Verwirrung des Gefühls" which befalls him when he loses this trust. For Kleist himself, "das Vertrauen" is "die erste Bedingung der Liebe;"[6] "Miss-trauen," on the other hand, is "die schwarze Sucht der Seele."[7] Carlos, in defending his bestowal of trust in Princess Eboli, tells Posa (paraphrased): "Glaube an menschliche Vortrefflichkeit ist der Seligkeiten göttlichste," (2369–70) and Posa himself calls "Misstrauen gegen den Freund" "der Schwächen schwächster." (3634–36) And Tasso, for all his problems with the concept of trust, conceives the possibility of giving oneself to another completely as a "Wollust, die schönste guter Menschen." (1285–87) A breach of trust, real or unreal, between the hero and his personal antagonist, forms the

---

5   For a discussion of this phenomenon, see: Wolfdietrich Rasch, *Freundschaftskult und Freundschaftsdichtung im deutschen Schrifttum des 18. Jahrhunderts* (Halle, 1936).

6   Letter to Wilhelmine von Zenge from the beginning of the year 1800.

7   DIE FAMILIE GHONOREZ, 515.

crucial stumbling block in each hero's development. The young man, because he has given himself completely to a trust bond with his dramatic partner, cannot withstand a forfeit of this confidence on the antagonist's part, and it propels him into inner chaos, and guilt. Precisely because the young hero has given his whole heart to a faith-friendship with his chosen guide, does the trust crisis have such a devastating effect on him.

Thus, Carlos', Tasso's and the Prince of Homburg's downfalls are the result, not of a simple, single event or an individual guilt, but of a complexity of factors; neither the young hero nor his environment, alone, is responsible for the young man's undoing, but both share a significant part of the blame for the dramatic entanglement. Initially, the hero's decline is essentially unwarranted as far as his own intentions are concerned, but as matters develop, the young man, too, becomes burdened with an unmistakable personal guilt, and it is as a reaction to this guilt that his final insight occurs.

### Insight

The moment of insight may be regarded as a return by the poets to the classical tradition in drama. At least in Goethe's and Schiller's plays, insight can readily be interpreted as a superimposition of the traditional dramatic outcome on the Storm and Stress play. At this moment the hero comes to terms with his fate; he recognizes a personal guilt along with an undeserved misfortune, he affirms his existence anyway, and the audience goes home reconciled. One can view each of the plays under discussion either as a tragedy or a non-tragedy, but even if one sees them as tragedies, they are mitigated tragedies, and their mitigated effect is derived from the moment of insight.

Insight for Carlos, Tasso, and the Prince of Homburg is a violent experience. In one memorable moment, always with the help of the personal antagonist, the heroes confront a new reality. They have no choice but to react because of the extreme situations in which they find themselves, and their reactions in each play amount to a sudden new awareness of themselves and their environment. All at once they are freed from the veil of confusion which surrounded them, are raised from their previous downcast states, and are faced with a new outlook from which there is no escape. There is no turning-back from this landmark, no avoiding the issue at hand, but they must each respond to the call of the moment as it is sounded. Their insights are traumatic awakenings with no alternative.

Posa's death is the liberating event in Carlos' development. In one horror-filled moment, Carlos is freed from his crippling passion and made ready to accept his nobler calling as the emancipator of man. Like a flame extinguished, Carlos' love for Elisabeth is snuffed out by his friend's sacrifice. To be sure, Carlos misinterprets Posa's motives to be purely friendship-oriented, but the effect is the same: with Posa's death, Carlos' past is put behind him and his thoughts are directed towards only one goal: to live henceforth in dedication to his friend's memory by carrying out the mission for which Posa had sacrificed his life.

Why is Carlos so susceptible to Posa's final action? Ultimately, friendship and basic noble character prove to be stronger in Carlos than the love for Elisabeth. One must remember that Carlos always was willing to be rehabilitated by his friend and that he had often allowed himself to be manipulated by both Posa and Elisabeth, but he had never had a real chance to escape himself because of the extraneous circumstances to which he always fell victim. Always, just at the moment when Carlos was about to conquer himself, he was thrust back into his passion by an unfortunate turn of events from outside. The last time it was Posa himself who diverted Carlos' good intentions. Only now, with Posa's ultimate sacrifice, does Carlos have a clear opportunity to become what he was always meant to be. Schiller, of course, made Carlos what he is, and since it was always Schiller's intent to have Carlos' noble nature win the struggle between inclination and duty, there was never any real question about the outcome of this transition-play. DON CARLOS is dedicated first of all to an idea, and because this idea only reaches its full fruition in the hero's final confession to it, Carlos *must* ultimately be converted. The heart of Schiller's message lies in the crown prince's regeneration.

While the beauty of Schiller's "Freiheitsdrama" is still captivating, there are certain weaknesses in the play that have long been recognized, and one of these weaknesses is the unpersuasive quality of Carlos' final transformation. It simply lacks credibility. It seems improbable that Carlos, the immature and impetuous young man, will now dedicate himself to a foreign goal, or that he will be able to pursue such a goal with some persistency. The character changes required of him are too great and too sudden. Not only must the crown prince renounce his love for Elisabeth, but he is also required to alter his basic nature and suddenly function from a purely intellectual base. Perhaps one difficulty in making this radical transition acceptable is that, as Gisela Heyn points out, Schiller does not have time to motivate Carlos' shift of attitude sufficiently.[8] Another possibility is that Schiller must *explain* Carlos' conversion in order to get his message across, and that adds to the credibility gap. Character changes are difficult enough to demonstrate on the stage, but when direct rational explanation is employed as

---

[8]    Miss Heyn writes: "Das Unbehagen, das der Zuschauer bei dieser Erklärung verspürt, muss wohl in erster Linie auf den Fehler in der dramatischen Ökonomie zurückgeführt werden, dass Posa, entgegen den ursprünglichen Plänen, zu viel Raum beansprucht und Carlos, als der Hauptgestalt, keine Zeit mehr bleibt, um seine Taten und Entschlüsse glaubhaft motivieren zu können." (Gisela Heyn, *Der junge Schiller als Psychologe* (Zürich, 1966), p. 52).

the medium for the message, the viewer is unable to assimilate the character transformation. It does not help, either, that Carlos himself is required to do the explaining, saying explicitly what his new beliefs are, and discarding his old person and accepting his new duties in so many words. While both of these are plausible reasons for the final weakness in Schiller's play, there is still a more basic reason for the flaw. Carlos' final insight is unconvincing as compared to Tasso's or the Prince of Homburg's insights primarily because Carlos does not ultimately come to terms with his own reality, but with Posa's. When Schiller moved from a Carlos-"Liebestragödie" to a Posa-"Humanitätsdrama," he imposed a foreign goal on Carlos, without changing Carlos' original character sufficiently in order for him to ultimately accept this goal. Schiller did not go back and recast Carlos to meet his new objective, and consequently, instead of only having to come to terms with his love for Elisabeth, as would be Carlos' task by nature and by Schiller's original intent, Carlos must assume a reality outside of himself in addition to relinquishing his love. The purpose of the drama is not for Carlos to become Carlos, but for Carlos to become Posa. So the ultimate weakness lies not in Carlos' intentions, which are good and genuine enough, but in a basic breach of purpose in Schiller's play.

Tasso's insight results from his great distress following the embrace of the Princess and the discovery of this act by the court group. In his despair, Tasso succumbs to a blasphemy of his entire surroundings, so appalling that even Antonio is shocked, and exclaims in wonder at the total estrangement of the poet from himself and all reality. Antonio's various and repeated admonitions gradually penetrate Tasso's consciousness in spite of Tasso's attempts to deflect them, the final warning breaks through the last remaining cloud of resistance, and Tasso recognizes in full clarity the truth of himself and his Ferrara situation. In one "Erkenne, was du bist!," the full weight of Tasso's life as a poet and its meaning in the outside world falls in on him, and he is helpless to resist the effect. Following an intuitive answer of "Ja, du erinnerst mich zur rechten Zeit!," the poet speaks the highly beautiful and ambiguous monologue which has inspired many varied interpretations. The immediate impression is that Tasso recognizes the consoling power of his talent; in thinking now about his creativity in light of his present misery, he sees it as a source of comfort which other men lack at such wretched times. Then, he also gives voice to the reason behind his present misery. Having already recognized his own guilt in the situation, he now also apprises the true nature of his tragedy as it stems from the unavoidable conflict between the poet and society. Distinguishing between himself and Antonio in symbolic terms, he describes his fate as an example of the everlasting tension between the creative and volatile artist on the one hand, and the tangibly active and stable man on the other. Tasso paints the full picture of his undoing, and if he does not completely affirm his tragic existence, he at least recognizes it now in unmasked truth, and that constitutes his final insight.

Tasso's problem has been that he could not accept the timeless gap which exists between the realm of the poet and the world of reality. His attempts to bridge this gap led inevitably to his downfall. Now, Tasso faces bleakly his tragic isolation, he admits his own folly in thinking that he could conquer the duality in his own life, and he accepts himself as a poet for the first time with no illusionary aids. Tasso cannot delude himself any further, and left with nothing but his poet's core, he reasserts himself in defense of his creative talent, reminding Antonio that the world allows for various kinds of existences. Actually, however, Tasso does no more than *comprehend* the true nature of his dilemma. He has no opportunity to alter his situation or to make amends for his former errors. He does not rise to glorious heights like Carlos or the Prince of Homburg, nor does he even have the chance to affirm his condition voluntarily; he is simply forced to last-minute renunciation of his past and to irrevocable insight. It has often been asserted that an essential part of the idea of "Humanität" is *voluntary* renunciation and acceptance of one's fate. I would dispute any argument that Carlos and the Prince of Homburg have more choice than Tasso about what finally happens to them, but at least Carlos and the Prince do have the option of choosing a course of action after their fates have been established, which the poet does not have. For this reason, TASSO strikes one as being the greatest tragedy. The poet is left with nothing but forced insight. Also, while Carlos and the Prince of Homburg ultimately rise above their antagonists in their final glory, Tasso is simply left clinging to Antonio's hand. There is no reconciliation between Tasso's and Antonio's worlds, simply desperate perception of the tragic gap.

The question of just how much TASSO is a tragedy is a greatly disputed one. Goethe called the play a "Schauspiel," and that gives justification to those who see in it hope for the poet's further survival. On the other hand, there are those who view the play as a stark tragedy. Like everyone else, I have no answer to what happens to Tasso after the concluding line. Moreover, I see basis for both kinds of interpretation. While there may be no final answers, I do want to add that, in contrast to Werther who ends by committing suicide, and Euphorion, who is destroyed before he reaches any real conception of his situation in the world, Tasso at least is brought to a definite insight of his wretchedness, and in this insight alone lies an alleviating effect to pure tragedy. At least Tasso learns to understand what his tragedy is all about.

The Prince of Homburg experiences nothing less than a spiritual rebirth when he receives the Elector's letter. From ravaging fear of death to personal choice of death, he is awakened to a new consciousness when he realizes that the Elector has given him the responsibility to decide his own fate. Kleist's hero does not need many words to convince the audience of his conversion; his manner alone in the scene with Natalie attests to the authenticity of his insight. The "awakening" scene in the Prince of Homburg is stylistically one of the most fascinating scenes in German literature. In more of a medley of gestures and half-phrases than the usual dramatic dialogue, and indicative of the subtle inner struggle between the two lovers, the Prince slowly grasps the meaning of the Elector's message, and suddenly the world changes color for him. Now in control of the greater consequences implied in the decision to live or die, all at once the threat of death disappears, and what was once a terrifying prospect turns into an acceptable, and even preferred, course of action. The Prince seems to know instinctively that he cannot dispute the Elector's decision, but that he must agree with it. There is no conscious weighing of alternatives for Kleist's hero, simply gradual absorption of a new reality. As Gerhard Fricke describes the insight, the Prince slowly "sinks" into awareness of his new situation.[9] So it is that Natalie's warnings of impending disaster fall on deaf ears. What only a few moments earlier would have created panic in the Prince, is now met with a smile. His pride and honor regained, not even pleas for personal consideration from his beloved can alter his new intentions. The irony of Homburg's insight is that, just at the moment when the threats to his life are conquerable, he rejects that possibility to adopt a position peculiar to his adversary. The Prince of Homburg's final insight is more extreme than either Carlos' or Tasso's because it includes the necessity to die.

Exactly what prompts Homburg's inner transformation is a matter of great conjecture and debate. It is generally known among Kleist followers how many different interpretations of this hero's final insight exist. These views vary from those critics who regard the outcome of the Prince's trial as a surrender of the individual to the law, to those who see in his conversion another example of a Kleistian triumph, through feeling, of the individual over outward threats to his person. Remaining with the basic facts that exist in the insight-scene, one finds that: 1. Homburg chooses to die rather than to live; therefore, outwardly at least, he accommodates to the demands of a reality outside of himself; and 2. he admits a selfguilt in the downfall process. Whether this guilt is related to his original error on the battlefield, or whether it stems from his loss of dignity in the fear-of-death scene and is bound up with his forfeit of trust in the Elector, or whether it is a guilt even more elusive to the reader, is not clear; what is established is that he recognizes and confesses a personal guilt at the moment of insight. These facts alone are enough to rank the PRINCE OF HOMBURG as a "Bildungsdrama" along with CARLOS and TASSO. Like these heroes, the Prince stumbles on the world around him and finally comes to terms with that world. Like them, he is neither completely innocent nor completely guilty in the fate that befalls him, and he ultimately recognizes and confesses a personal share in his undoing. The tendency of Kleist's play, like that of Schiller's and that of

---

[9] Fricke, *op.cit.,* p. 190f.

Goethe's, is to place two realities in opposition to one another, and then, through a complex set of dramatic circumstances, to lead the one reality to a final recognition of, and accommodation with, the other reality, or, in more concrete terms, to educate the young man to the exigencies of his life. Kleist's drama is an even more pronounced "Bildungsdrama" than TASSO, because, on the surface at least, Kleist's hero, like Carlos, submits finally to his external reality, while Tasso, as the poet, is spared assimilation into his outside world in order to preserve the dignity and equal validity of his poet's existence. Different from both Schiller's and Goethe's young men, however, is the almost ecstatic posture with which the Prince of Homburg finally meets his fate. Still a Kleistian hero, the Prince finds renewed oneness in his person at the conclusion of his experience, and this feeling is relayed to the audience as part of the proof of his changed psyche. The Prince is also the only one of the three heroes who finally gets what he was dreaming about. While Carlos must renounce his claims to personal happiness to accept Posa's legacy, and Tasso also loses everything dear to him, the Prince of Homburg is ultimately awarded his original goal. A second great irony in Homburg's "Bildungsprozess" is that, after he has suffered the most of the three protagonists to learn about his reality, even having to choose his own death in the process, like a comic reversal he is granted his wishes at the end. Whether he actually still wants them or can accept them at this moment, or whether, as one critic, Elsbeth Leber, believes, the ending of Kleist's drama is the first real tragic moment of the play, is another debatable question.[10]

One lesson that all three of our young men learn is that there is no room for boundless action in their worlds. The price of such nonconformity is severe; death in Carlos' and the Prince of Homburg's environments, and in Tasso's gentler setting, at least banishment. The heroes learn this truth, they learn to face the harsh realities of their lives, and still, finally, each, in varying degrees, affirms his own existence. One thing that distinguishes our stage hero from his modern successors is that our protagonist still perceives a world order in which the individual has a personal responsibility to preserve himself for his manifest role in society. He may fall victim to an unjust fate, he may even become burdened with an involuntary guilt, but yet, in the end, he does not withdraw from his surroundings, sink into damning despair, or become simply a passive victim, but he accepts his lot, and essentially he says yes to his life. He does not deny all self-participation in his destiny, but recognizes a personal guilt at the conclusion of his trouble, and he voices this awareness publicly as part of his final insight. Our young man, in contrast to the modern hero, still feels that his life is important in his milieu and that his actions have some ultimate meaning.

10  Leber, *op.cit.,* e.g. p. 136.

Therefore, although he learns about the tragic gap in his society and that this gap cannot be reconciled in his own life or to his own benefit, he still affirms his being and remains noble at the end.

A fitting indication that the three heroes have reached maturity is that they each remove a type of mask at the conclusion of the plays. Carlos removes a real mask, Tasso sheds his mask of self-delusion, and the Prince of Homburg is freed from a blindfold. At these moments the young men face different fates, but they all have in common a matured perspective.

### The "Teachers"

Carlos, Tasso, and the Prince of Homburg do not reach insight unassisted, but with the help of two supporting characters in each play who act as "teachers" to the young men. There is in each of our dramas a triangle-configuration resembling the "love-friendship" triangle so often encountered in the literature of the eighteenth century, of which the Werther-Lotte-Albert triangle is a prime example.[11] In our "Bildungsdramen," this threesome has a somewhat different function. The problem here is not one woman caught between two men; the woman, though loved, is only an auxiliary figure to a larger problem. The trio is structured to "educate" the young hero to the realities of his life, and the male antagonist and the beloved woman play paramount roles in the development process. Through both positive and negative, intentional and unintentional means, they help the hero to identify his proper calling in life, to find his particular place in society. The themes of love and conflict are highly entwined in these plays, and it is the combination of push and pull forces by the male and female "teachers" in the triangular arrangement, which ultimately leads to the hero's "Bildung."

### The Personal Antagonist

Within the general context of the court, which is antagonistic too, each of our young men is faced with a personal antagonist whose main task it is to finally raise the hero to maturity. These male opponents are opposites in nature to the impulsive, temperamental young men. They are older than the heroes, experienced in life, certain of themselves and their own roles in the world, and they each represent the sphere to which the hero must finally accommodate.

---

[11] For other examples, and a general discussion of this phenomenon, see: Ladislao Mittler, "Freundschaft und Liebe in der deutschen Literatur des 18. Jahrhunderts," *Stoffe, Formen, Strukturen,* eds. Albert Fuchs and Helmut Motekat (München, 1962), 97–138.

Although the personal antagonists are open to human error, they are generally objective and deliberate in their actions, and they look outside of themselves when making their decisions. Their world is the public domain, and they all have a responsible role in society. These qualities tend to make them appropriate "teachers" for the young men, who, in turn, within the antagonist relationship, focus on their opposites as chosen leaders for them. It is interesting that in each play the hero is without parents and that a bond with the antagonist serves as a substitute for parental guidance and love. The young men want and need an intimate relationship with their adversaries, and their efforts to create or maintain such a bond are part of the reason for their downfalls. The antagonists do not require emotional ties to their youthful companions. They are more impersonal in their human relationships, and they are even capable of using others to their own ends, and to some extent they all do this with our young men. The antagonists are complex figures; they have dual roles assigned to them in that they are not only instrumental in the hero's final insight, but they also all contribute in large part to his downfall. This is most true in Tasso's case, where Antonio is the only overt impetus to the poet's undoing; for Carlos and the Prince of Homburg, the general court establishments bear the primary burden for the initial impacts. The antagonists in our dramas are usurpers of the young men as well as their eventual saviors. Their negative influence is seen most clearly in the fact that, in each play, it is at their instigation that the hero at some point is arrested and imprisoned. Symbolically, one might say that they take possession of the hero's physical person with this act, just as later, at the moment of insight, they might be accused of capturing his mind. And yet these antagonists do not fit the usual image of the dramatic antagonist. Because these dramas are "Bildungsdramen," and because a large part of the antagonist's job is to raise the hero finally to maturity, Posa, Antonio, and the Elector do not conform to the usual idea of the antagonist as possessing qualities directly opposite from the admirable traits of the hero, as the evil force opposing the hero's will, but, in each play, although they have an undesirable side as well, these figures are essentially "good," with a good influence in the heroes' lives. Ultimately, they act as supporters to the young men, as models to be emulated at the moment of crisis, and because of this, the authors are careful to present them as worthy figures, to always portray their sides of the dramatic conflicts as well, and with equal fairness. There is a balance in these plays between the worlds of the heroes and the worlds of the antagonists, and these worlds are brought into final juncture when the heroes reach maturity.

One should not think of the educational process from the side of the antagonist as a continuous, conscious and intentional undertaking. With the exception of Posa, who does proceed to change Carlos deliberately, the antagonists are mostly unaware of their educational role in the heroes' lives. They act as unpremeditated catalysts at the moment of insight. Of course it is true that unplanned involvement lies in the nature of all drama, but there is another good reason why these antagonists would not try to influence the heroes directly. We are talking here about male relationships, on a level and in circumstances where some degree of natural rivalry would have to be present. It is unlikely that the heroes, in spite of admiration for, and the need of acceptance by their adversaries, would respond to conscious manipulation. We see how Tasso and the Prince of Homburg react instinctively to any deliberate control by Antonio and the Elector. Tasso, as soon as Antonio tries to reform him in the duel scene, aggressively defends his poet's ways, and the Prince of Homburg rejects the Elector's treatment proudly at the time of his arrest. Even Posa chooses for the most part to work through Elisabeth to accomplish his objectives with Carlos. And at the moment of insight, when the antagonists, like the heroes, have no choice but to do something vis-a-vis their youthful opponents, they do not attack the hero's person directly, they do not say: you are wrong, change!, but in each case they cleverly appeal to the young man's sense of honor, they use tactics, in other words, which will work psychologically between males to effect the hero's insight.

The approach of protagonist and antagonist at the moment of insight is in a way symbolic of the idea of "Humanität" in the Age of Goethe. Part of the ideal of "Humanität" is "wholeness," reconciliation of opposites into harmony, and if one views these characters as antitheses, then their final meeting represents an abstraction of sorts of the qualities of the one by the other. One might well claim, as has frequently been done, that these characters are insufficient in themselves and that only when united would they make a whole. The protagonists certainly need some of the wisdom and temperance of their counselors, and the antagonists would do well to capture or recapture some of the purity of their youthful comrades. In the final moments of the play, at the moment of insight, such a synthesis is simulated. To be sure, the hero approaches the antagonist more at this moment than vice-versa — that is the "Bildungs"-sense of the plays, but, still, the antagonist, too, is affected by the sudden turn of events. Unlike the court environments, which do not change at all, the antagonist does learn *something* from his experience with his vexatious junior, and conveys this by a final stance, and this mutual accommodation symbolizes the complete human being aspired to by the tenders of "Humanität."

The protagonist-antagonist relationship between Carlos and Posa has friendship as its base, but the friendship is not in balance. For Carlos the friendship is pure; for Posa it has a purpose. Posa needs Carlos politically to secure his plan to liberate the Netherlands, and is willing to go to any lengths to achieve his goal. When he returns to Madrid and finds Carlos consumed by his passion for Elisabeth, he proceeds immediately to use Carlos' love to reestablish his interest in the humanitarian ideals, and nothing, even the failure of Carlos' interview with his father and the resulting danger from the Eboli-intrigue, diverts Posa from his intentions to reform Carlos and to use him as the vehicle for accomplishing his political mission. In the end he even arranges his own death to redirect Carlos.

In comparing Carlos and Posa, one is inclined to think of Carlos as the person who reacts from his feelings of the moment, and in that sense selfishly, and it is easy to credit Posa with unselfish, humanitarian motives. But in a real sense, Posa is more selfish than Carlos. Posa is fanatically selfish about *his* ideas, noble as they may be, and the ruthlessness with which he is willing to carry out his *private* reformation exposes him as not completely selfless. His political fanaticism causes him to act toward the people around him in such a way as to jeopardize the very freedom for which he crusades. The way he manipulates Carlos shows this, and even Schiller recognizes that Posa's idealism turns him into something of a despot.[12] Posa's death is also part of his fanaticism. Although other measures are open to him at the crucial moment, Posa deliberately chooses that means by which he can best show his complete dedication to his ideals: as Schiller says:

> Er stirbt, um für sein — in des Prinzen Seele niedergelegtes — Ideal alles zu tun und zu geben, was ein Mensch für etwas tun und geben kann, das ihm das Teuerste ist; um ihm auf die nachdrücklichste Art, die er in seiner Gewalt hat, zu zeigen, wie sehr er an die Wahrheit und Schönheit dieses Entwurfes glaube und wie wichtig die Erfüllung desselben sei.[13]

From the point of view of character development, it is interesting to observe how Carlos and Posa exchange roles behaviorally in the course of the play, how Posa's character begins to suffer as he becomes more and more involved politically, while at the same time, and to at least an equal degree, Carlos' character begins to grow. Posa's noble dream becomes tainted with grandiose delusions. That he contemplates sacrificing Carlos for the king shows this, and also his decision to solve the Eboli-complications alone instead of informing Carlos of his secret dealings with Philipp is motivated by hubris. At the end of the play, despite Posa's oftentimes shabby treatment of Carlos, Carlos is willing to give his life for his friend for no other reason than personal friendship; Posa would be incapable of such selflessness. It is also Carlos who finally redeems the dream by his conversion to it, and, as E. L. Stahl points out, Carlos is the one and only character in the play who grows in stature.[14] Carlos never fully understands Posa, he remains naive and selfless in his love for his friend to the end, and this purity makes it possible for Posa's death to have the desired effect on Carlos.

---

12  BRIEFE ÜBER DON CARLOS, elfter Brief.
13  *Ibid.*, zwölfter Brief.
14  *Friedrich Schiller's Drama. Theory and Practice, op. cit.*, p. 34.

It would be difficult to describe the antagonism between Tasso and Antonio without quoting or paraphrasing what Wolfdietrich Rasch has already said in such detail.[15] For the most part I agree with him. The antagonism, while real enough, is subtle and difficult to define. It exists to some degree quite naturally because of the confined environment and the competing roles in which the characters are cast. Most of all, however, these two men have completely different natures, which makes them uncomfortable in each other's presence and overly sensitive to each other's significance at Ferrara's court. Although Tasso is the one in need of recognition by his society, it is Antonio, with his annoyance at finding the poet the center of attention when he returns from Rome, who precipitates the duel scene. Antonio's disdain of the poet reveals itself openly when Tasso approaches and offers his friendship, and Antonio's scornful rejection of this gesture leads to an exchange of insults and rebuttals that ends in the drawing of swords. Rasch's description of the duel scene shows how inevitable and how rooted in basic personality differences the hostility is:

> Es ist, zugespitzt gesagt, ein gegenstandsloser Streit. Keiner hat dem anderen vorher etwas getan, was zum Zusammenstoss führen müsste. Tassos Verhalten gibt Antonio keinen Anlass, ihn zu kränken. Aber gerade dieser gegenstandslose Streit, wie Goethe sich ihn entwickeln lässt, charakterisiert die Art dieses Konflikts, der im Grunde aus der Verschiedenheit der Naturen stammt, aus dem Gegensatz des Wesens. Die blosse Existenz des einen scheint den anderen zu stören. Aus dem Dasein selbst, dem Nebeneinander der beiden Männer entfaltet sich der Konflikt wie eine Ausstrahlung ihres Wesens.[16]

The poet in Hofmannsthal's sketch also touches the core of the Tasso-Antonio conflict when he says: "Tasso und Antonio: ja sie sind einander bis zur Auflösung gefährlich, indem sie bloss da sind."[17]

Antonio has a double function in TASSO which makes his character controversial. He is both the representative of the world against which Tasso flounders, and in that role he must be presented positively in order to carry out his final function as inspirational leader to Tasso, and at the same time he is the impetus to the poet's downfall. In our other plays, the antagonist has a less direct role in the hero's undoing. Antonio, acting as *both* destroyer and savior, is required to shift from the first role to the second so hurriedly as to cause apparent inconsistencies in his character. Rasch explains Antonio's delicate and double task in terms of the nature of TASSO, the drama of the poet.[18] A poet's

---

[15]  *Goethes "Torquato Tasso". Die Tragödie des Dichters, op.cit.*, esp. p. 81f.
[16]  *Ibid.*, p. 93.
[17]  Hugo von Hofmannsthal, "Unterhaltung über den 'Tasso' von Goethe." *Ausgewählte Werke*, Vol. 2 (Frankfurt a.M., 1957), p. 434.
[18]  *Goethes "Torquato Tasso" Die Tragödie des Dichters, op.cit.*, p. 90f.

conflict with his society is necessarily a refined, psychological struggle rather than an open, external clash, and it would be improper to portray Tasso as the victim of a more overt intrigue acceptable in other dramas. Everything in TASSO, beginning with the laureation as the precipitating event to the poet's problems and ending with a banishment instead of death, is presented in a subdued and reserved tone to harmonize with the portrayal of the poet, and Antonio's dual casting is part of this general need for sophistication.

Where I disagree with Rasch is in his evaluation of Antonio's final change of attitude toward Tasso. Rasch maintains that what brings about Antonio's transformation is the intensity of Tasso's love for the Princess, which causes the poet to jeopardize his whole existence at Ferrara.[19] I do not think that it is Tasso's love as such that impresses Antonio in the embrace scene — that seems to narrow the interpretation too much; rather I believe that Antonio at this moment sees only a person in great need, and that the indisputability and the depth of Tasso's distress then brings out the human side of Antonio. Antonio had never taken Tasso seriously before, he had always considered him to be a superficial person who used his sensitivity as a means of eliciting the sympathy of the court, but who was still clever enough to preserve his advantages. Now Antonio sees that he misjudged Tasso, that Tasso's actions are genuine, and that the intensity of his feelings are driving him to self-destruction. And at this moment, when all rivalry falls away and the poet stands before him in utter desolation, Antonio takes another look, and for the first time the Duke's admonition that he should be a friend and counselor to Tasso takes on meaning. Antonio, for whom the poet's world had never been worthy of serious consideration, now reaches into this very world for the means to bring Tasso to his senses.

The real antagonist of the Prince of Homburg is the law of the state of Brandenburg, the Elector is only its chief administrator. As the highest representative and defender of the law, the Elector has no choice but to arrest the Prince when he disobeys orders on the battlefield. In spite of the fact that the Elector loves the Prince and does not want to harm him, and although he probably anticipates some protest from the Prince's fellow-officers, it does not occur to the Elector to make an exception to the law, even for the Prince. The Prince is guilty by law, and must be punished as the law prescribes; these are the realities of the society of Brandenburg. The Elector is even more committed to the law by his own hasty announcement of the death verdict, before he knows that the Prince is the evil-doer.

---

[19]  *Ibid.*, p. 166f.

The Elector is undoubtedly one of the most ambiguous figures in all of German literature. One never knows what he is thinking, but neither does one have to know, because his actions are always determined by a necessity outside of himself. What the Elector wants for himself is never a main issue, he must always act as executor of the higher dictates of Brandenburg. This is true not only at the time of the Prince's initial offense, but it also motivates the Elector's fateful letter to the Prince. Again later, the Elector has no choice as to how he will react when he learns of the Prince's disgraceful behavior in not accepting the established consequences of his wrongdoing. His hands are tied once more, and this time he must depend on the Prince himself for the solution to the problem. Here the Elector is caught in the dilemma of either executing or pardoning a coward, which means that he cannot act at all toward the Prince until he rehabilitates him. When the Elector arrested the Prince, it was to insure against a repetition of such violations of the law, and only if the Prince recognizes and accepts his guilt, i.e. only if he himself endorses the law, does this action have any validity for the state. To execute him as a coward would not only be meaningless as far as the law is concerned, but it would also tend to make a martyr of him and a tyrant of the Elector. Better even to let him run free in his cowardice than to execute him. And the Elector cannot pardon the Prince either, because he can only pardon a partner in the law. Only if the Prince recognizes and accepts his guilt, i.e. only if he sanctions the authority of the law, would pardon be thinkable. So the Elector must refer to the Prince himself for the answer to the dilemma. He must first restore him to himself before he can act at all. And the Elector obviously believes that he can restore the Prince and bring him to his senses. In writing the letter, the Elector does not actually place the law in jeopardy, because, knowing and believing in the Prince as he does, he can predict the reaction to the letter. What the Elector has to find out from Natalie, and what astonishes him, is that the Prince did not endorse his decision from the beginning. Only now, when he learns this, does the Elector realize that the Prince has never thought about his deed in terms of the law, that he has never perceived his own guilt. The Elector's letter — shifting responsibility for the law to the Prince — is intended to make the Prince see his own problem in terms of the state of Brandenburg, and the Elector is confident the outcome.

The PRINCE OF HOMBURG reveals the same kind of break in the middle from the standpoint of the personal antagonist as do CARLOS and TASSO. Like in the other plays, there is, toward the end of the second act, a shift of emphasis from protagonist to antagonist, where the antagonist assumes a position of at least equal importance to the hero. As in the other plays, it might also be possible to show that the author's sympathies shift at this point to the antagonist's side. From the shift forward, the problem focuses on making the hero accommodate to the demands of the antagonist's world. In all of these plays, the third act serves as a kind of new exposition.

In analysing the protagonist-antagonist relationships in the three dramas, one sees that the influence of the antagonist on the hero is not evenly distributed; it begins for the most part weakly, (with the exception of Posa) is not a conscious force, and gains momentum until the point of insight at the end.

## The Beloved Woman

The women, Elisabeth, Princess Leonore, and Natalie, like the antagonists, play an important role in the young mens' development, but their influence is exerted in a different way. The beloved woman plays her role consciously and by choice, and her efforts extend throughout the play. The woman is largely responsible for the young man's problem; his attraction to her causes the initial collision between hero and court. Although the woman's dramatic role is secondary in comparison to that of the hero or the personal antagonist, she occupies a central position inasmuch as the action revolves largely around her person. The woman is the intermediary between the young man and the antagonist; she works for the approach of the hero toward the antagonist-world. In doing so, she is working toward a renunciation of herself, for she knows that the love is impossible or difficult to achieve, either because it is socially prohibited, as in CARLOS and TASSO, or because of the situational difficulties, as in the PRINCE OF HOMBURG. The woman has no selfish motives in promoting the young man's "Bildung." She loves and wants to help him, and she uses the emotional bond between them to work in his behalf. The direction of the plot is that the antagonist-world intervenes in this love relationship. Initially, the young man is pure, like the woman, and reacts to the voice of his heart. As the action develops, the young man must take on complexity, move toward the antagonist, and lose his purity. The beloved woman sees the necessity for this and influences him in this direction.

All of the women are mature, self-possessed individuals, and are equal if not superior to the men they love. They are capable of influencing their surroundings and they have an ennobling influence on the young men which amounts to a "Bildungsmacht."[20] Elisabeth and the Princess have the qualities of the idealized image of woman in the Age of Goethe. They are sophisticated, strongly virtuous women, and an important part of their beings is their exemplary stature. Much of their influence on the young men consists of direct sermons about proper behavior. There are also the mother-figure overtones in their relationships to the young men, and there is the question of how much they are loved for themselves or as images of womanhood. Elisabeth says herself

---

20  The old man in Goethe's MÄRCHEN says: "Die Liebe herrscht nicht, aber sie bildet, und das ist mehr." Tasso, following the scene with the Princess in which she confesses her love, soliloquizes: "Ihr bin ich, bildend soll sie mich besitzen." (1159)

that Carlos loves her because he cannot have her (780–82). The Princess is unattainable for Tasso and lives in the other world toward which he strives. Natalie, though younger than the other women and belonging mostly to a later generation of women, equals Elisabeth and the Princess in her pervasive moral strength. She is also conspicuously superior to her young man in emotional control and the ability to interpret reality and adjust to it. All of the women undergo their own struggles between inclination and duty, they learn to renounce, and they act as models for the young men who must also learn to disclaim personal inclination and accept an imposed fate. One tends to like these women because they are not exactly perfect, not flawless like Iphigenie who is the purest example of the "Humanitätsideal." These women are more human than Iphigenie, and at the same time more vulnerable. Even Elisabeth, who is Schiller's idea of the "schöne Seele," is by no means saintly. She undergoes personal struggles and shows that she is possibly guilt-prone as she moves away from her loyalty to Philipp and gets caught up in Posa's plans.

Elisabeth fits perfectly the role of go-between between Carlos and Posa, embodying as she does the finer qualities of both men — some of the "Gefühlsmensch" that is Carlos, some of the idealist that is Posa — without the weaknesses that are inherent in the extremes of these qualities. Elisabeth cooperates from the beginning in helping Posa reform Carlos. She wants very much to help Carlos because she loves him, and she sees the need for Carlos to overcome his passion and to assume his proper calling as crown prince. In her first meeting with Carlos, even before she knows Posa's specific intentions, she succeeds in re-directing Carlos' interests to the political ideals for which Posa crusades. Elisabeth is a woman of great compassion and great courage. She is naturally sympathetic to the people in the Netherlands, and she is willing to risk her own safety to help to liberate them. Even when she learns that Posa plans open rebellion, she is not frightened away, but promises her tacit support. Finally, she is even willing to give herself to Carlos to insure the realization of the Flanders mission. Backof points out how Elisabeth experiences the opposite spiritual development from Carlos in the course of the play. The farther Carlos moves away from his passion, the more Elisabeth tends to acquiesce in her love.[21] Philipp himself is of course most responsible for Elisabeth's alienation from the court, weakening her loyalty by his own ill-treatment of her, and then climaxing this behavior with his brutal murder of Posa.

On Tasso's long and downward road to disaster, the Princess is positive in only a negative way, in the way she pushes Tasso step by step toward his tragedy and recognition of his reality. During the process, the Princess truly tries to help

---

[21] Fritz Backof, *Schillers DON CARLOS und das Problem der Leidenschaft*, Diss. (Erlangen, 1925), p. 52.

Tasso find peace with himself and his environment, but she actually contributes more to his detriment than his well-being. She loves the poet and identifies more with his spirit and nature than anyone else at Ferrara, and she sees the need for mediation in his behalf, but her efforts only get Tasso more and more emotionally involved in his struggle. The Princess, for one thing, is guilty of either poor reasoning or poor judgment in the way she tries to bring Tasso and Antonio together and she recognizes this herself later (1670f). She was in a position to prepare Antonio for the meeting with Tasso, which she did not do even though she knew that Antonio was in a bad mood for reconciliation. Also, later, when she agrees to Leonore's plan to allow Tasso to leave Ferrara, she does so against her own personal desires to have Tasso stay, and without consulting Tasso before making the decision. Thirdly, the Princess allows Tasso to sit with his emotional problems in room arrest without giving him the slightest sign of her moral sympathy or of her continuing love. The way in which the Princess shows her love is debilitating to Tasso's nature from the beginning. She shows and withdraws it alternately, as if she had a fear of giving it at all. Extending the possibility of her love inflames and blinds Tasso in his relation to reality, withdrawing the signs of her love depresses and infuriates him. Tasso's hasty approach to Antonio and also the unpremeditated embrace are, in part, the result of her vacillation. So the Princess is essentially a negative force for Tasso, not only in her love, but also in her attempt to mediate Tasso's problems. Her failure to mediate adds to the degree of Tasso's tragedy. The tragic irony is that Tasso's approach to the other world, which is what the Princess wanted all along, happens only after she has abandoned him.

Natalie has one main function, and that is to effect a reconciliation between the Prince and the Elector. In contrast to Elisabeth and the Princess, who have broader roles and whose characters are exposed in more detail through dialogue by secondary figures, we know Natalie only in the context of her love for the Prince, and it is the persistency and the selflessness of this love which finally accomplishes the reconciliation. True reconciliation with the Elector requires of the Prince that he accept a verdict of death, as the course of Brandenburg justice requires it of him, and Natalie works for this, but she is also intent on *saving* the Prince's life and even is willing, as a last resort, to violate the Brandenburg code herself.[22] When it is crucial, Natalie seems always to be working against herself, but she manages the contradiction very well with the sheer strength of the love and the compassion she has for the Prince and the understanding she has for the Elector. In the fear-of-death scene, when the Prince treats her shamefully and actually abandons her outright, she responds magnanimously with only the

---

[22] Natalie makes herself guilty of a crime as punishable as the Prince's when she uses the Elector's name falsely to order Kottwitz and his troops into the city.

Prince's problem in mind, giving him back some of his composure and balance, and actually reorienting him enough so that the Elector's letter can have the proper impact. Natalie becomes directly responsible for this letter, which is the key to the Prince's insight, when she informs the Elector of the Prince's collapse. In the insight-scene, Natalie painfully plays out her contradictory role, opposing the Prince's awakening because she fears for his life, but it is just Natalie's opposition which leads the Prince to clarity about himself and to redemptive reconciliation with the Elector.

So the three separate conflicts are resolved by the antagonist and the beloved woman together. Posa influences Carlos deliberately in search of a higher goal and Elisabeth assists him. Antonio demoralizes Tasso, the Princess in spite of her good intentions only adds to the process, and then at the breaking point Antonio reacts sympathetically to save Tasso. The Elector with his legal limitations first causes the Prince's dilemma and then liberates him from it, and Natalie has the guiding hand in bringing about this liberation and insight.

# CONCLUSION

The Bildungsroman occupies an important place in literature, but the idea that a significant maturation process can exist also in drama has been recongnized in only a very limited way, if at all. This study has shown that such Bildungsdrama was produced in German literature, growing out of and extending beyond the period of Storm and Stress. Three plays from the Age of Goethe, Schiller's DON CARLOS, Goethe's TORQUATO TASSO, and Kleist's PRINZ FRIEDRICH VON HOMBURG, were taken as points of arrival in tracing the literary image of the Young Man, from an unteachable figure in Storm and Stress to a teachable one in these three Bildungsdramen.

The conclusion is reached that a valid comparison can be drawn between the Bildungsroman and a Bildungsdrama which appeared simultaneously on the literary scene in Germany, in the latter half of the eighteenth century. In accomplishing its function, the Bildungsdrama is necessarily limited in time and scope. Bildung is less obvious and discernable and happens quickly in a moment of self-recognition, but it is the main purpose of the author to show this insight on the part of the hero, and this intention and the fact that insight does occur in the drama, however short the process, makes it equatable with the like process in the Roman.

# BIBLIOGRAPHY

*Drama Theory*

Hamburger, Käte. *Die Logik der Dichtung.* 2d ed. Stuttgart, 1968.
Mandel, Oscar. *A Definition of Tragedy.* New York, 1961.
Staiger, Emil. *Grundbegriffe der Poetik.* Zürich, 1946.


*Eighteenth Century*

Hermann, Klaus, and Joachim Müller (eds.). *Sturm und Drang – Ein Lesebuch für unsere Zeit.* Berlin and Weimar, 1967.
Hoffmann, Therese. *Das klassisch-frühromantische Frauenideal,* Diss., Leipzig, 1932.
Ives Margaret C. "The Problem of Identity in German Tragedy between 1770 and 1808, "*Publications of the English Goethe Society,* XXXVI (1966), 34–59.
Jappe, Hajo. *Jugend deutschen Geistes. Das Bild des Jünglings in der Blüte der deutschen Dichtung (Klopstock bis Hölderlin).* Berlin, 1939.
Klein, J. "'Nathan,' 'Iphigenie,' 'Don Carlos' Bemerkungen zum vor- und frühklassischen Drama," *Wirkendes Wort,* VIII (1957/1958), 77–84.
Kluckhohn, Paul. *Die Auffassung der Liebe im 18. Jahrhundert und in der Romantik.* Halle (Saale), 1931.
– *Die Idee des Menschen in der Goethezeit.* Stuttgart, 1946.
Korff, H. A. *Geist der Goethezeit.* 5 vols. Leipzig, 1923–58.
Mittler, Ladislao. "Freundschaft und Liebe in der deutschen Literatur des 18. Jahrhunderts," in *Stoffe, Formen, Strukturen,* eds. Albert Fuchs and Helmut Motekat. München, 1962, 97–138.
Nohl, Herman. "Der Bildungsbegriff des Klassischen," *Sammlung,* IV (1949), 282–91.
Pascal, R. "The 'Sturm und Drang' Movement," *Modern Language Review,* XLVII (April, 1952), 129–51.
Rasch, Wolfdietrich. *Freundschaftskult und Freundschaftsdichtung im deutschen Schrifttum des 18. Jahrhunderts.* Halle, 1936.
Ruprecht, Erich. "Die Idee der Humanität in der Goethezeit," *Studium generale,* XV (1962), 179–201.
Schneider, F. J. *Die deutsche Dichtung der Geniezeit.* Stuttgart, 1952.
Sengle, Friedrich. "Klassik im deutschen Drama," in *Arbeiten zur deutschen Literatur 1750 bis 1850.* Stuttgart, 1965, 71–87.
Stahl, E. L. *Die religiöse und die humanitätsphilosophische Bildungsidee und die Entstehung des deutschen Bildungsromans im 18. Jahrhundert.* Bern, 1934.
Trunz, Erich. "Seelische Kultur. Eine Betrachtung über Freundschaft, Liebe und Familiengefühl im Schrifttum der Goethezeit," *Deutsche Vierteljahresschrift,* XXIV (1950), 214–42.
Wiese, Benno von. "Das Humanitätsideal in der deutschen Klassik," *Germanisch-Romanische Monatsschrift,* XX (1932), 321–33.

*Schiller*

*Werke.* ed. Eduard von der Hellen. 16 vols. Stuttgart and Berlin, 1904–05.
*Briefe.* ed. Fritz Jonas. 7 vols. Stuttgart, 1892–96.
Appelbaum Graham, Ilse. "The Structure of the Personality in Schiller's Tragic Poetry," in *Schiller. Bicentenary Lectures.* ed. F. Norman. London, 1960, 104–44.
Backof, Fritz. *Schillers 'Don Carlos' und das Problem der Leidenschaft.* Diss., Erlangen, 1925.
Beck, Adolf. "Die Krisis des Menschen im Drama des jungen Schiller," in *Forschung und Deutung.* Bonn, 1966, 119–66.
Buchwald, Reinhard. *Schiller.* 2 vols. Leipzig, 1937.
Cohn, Hilde D. "Gefängnis und Gefangenschaft in Schillers 'Don Carlos'," in *Festschrift für Bernhard Blume.* Göttingen, 1967, 81–89.
Gerhard, Melitta. *Schiller.* Bern, 1950.
Gronicka, André von. "Friedrich Schiller's Marquis Posa: A Character Study," *Germanic Review,* XXVI (1951), 196–214.
Heyn, Gisa. *Der junge Schiller als Psychologe.* Zürich, 1966.
Kaufmann, F. W. "Schuldverwicklung in Schillers Dramen," in *Schiller 1759–1959.* ed. John R. Frey. U. of Illinois Press, 1959, 76–104.
Luther, Bernhard. "Don Carlos und Hamlet," *Euphorion,* XII (1905), 561–72.
Müller, Joachim. "Der Held und sein Gegenspieler in Schillers Dramen," *Wissenschaftliche Zeitschrift der Universität Jena. Gesellschafts- und sprachwissenschaftliche Reihe,* IV/V (1958/1959), 451–69.
Stahl, E. L. *Friedrich Schiller's Drama. Theory and Practice.* Oxford, 1954.
Storz, Gerhard. *Der Dichter Friedrich Schiller.* Stuttgart, 1959.
– "Die Struktur des Don Carlos," *Jahrbuch der Schiller-Gesellschaft,* IV (1960), 110–39.
Wertheim, Ursula. *Schillers "Fiesko" und "Don Carlos". Zu Problemen des historischen Stoffes.* Weimar, 1958.
Wiese, Benno von. *Friedrich Schiller.* Stuttgart, 1959.


*Goethe*

*Werke.* ed. Eduard von der Hellen. 40 vols. Stuttgart, 1902.
Blumenthal, Liselotte. "Die Tasso-Handschriften," *Goethe,* neue Folge des Jahrbuchs der Goethe-Gesellschaft, XII (1950), 89–125.
Böckmann, Paul. "Goethes Bild des Dichters," in *Formensprache.* Hamburg, 1966, 106–25.
Burckhardt, Sigurd. "The Consistency of Goethe's *Tasso,*" *Journal of English and Germanic Philology,* LVII (1958), 394–402.
Forster, Leonard. "Thoughts on Tasso's Last Monologue," in *Essays in German Language, Culture and Society.* University of London: Institute of Germanic Studies, 1969, 18–23.
Hofmannsthal, Hugo von. "Unterhaltung über den 'Tasso' von Goethe," *Ausgewählte Werke II.* Frankfurt a.M.: Fischer, 1957, 428–39.
Linden, Walther. "Die Lebensprobleme in Goethes 'Tasso'," *Zeitschrift für Deutschkunde,* XLI (1927), 337–55.
Papst, Edmund. "Doubt, Certainty and Truth: Tasso's Vision of Reality," *Publications of the English Goethe Society,* XXXIV (1964), 122–52.
Peacock, Ronald. *Goethe's Major Plays.* Manchester, 1959.
"Goethe's Version of Poetic Drama," *Publications of the English Goethe Society,* XVI (1946), 29–53.

Rasch, Wolfdietrich. *Goethes "Torquato Tasso" Die Tragödie des Dichters.* Stuttgart, 1954.
Seidlin, Oskar. "Goethe's *Iphigenia* and the Humane Ideal," in *Goethe. A Collection of Critical Essays,* ed. Victor Lange. Prentice-Hall, 1968, 50–64.
Silz, Walter, "Ambivalences in Goethe's 'Tasso'," *Germanic Review,* XXXI (1956), 243–68.
Sthal, E. L. "Tasso's Tragedy and Salvation," in *Willoughby Miscellaneous.* Oxford, 1952, 191–203.
–   (ed.). *Torquato Tasso.* Oxford, 1962.
Staiger, Emil. *Goethe.* 3 vols. Zürich, 1952/1956/1959.
Wilkinson, Elizabeth M. "Goethe's 'Tasso'. The Tragedy of a Creative Artist," *Publications of the English Goethe Society,* XV (1945), 96–127.
–   "Tasso–ein gesteigerter Werther in the Light of Goethe's Principle of Steigerung," *Modern Language Review,* XLIV (1949), 305–28.
Wolff, Hans M. *Goethes Weg zur Humanität.* München, 1951.


*Kleist*


*Werke und Briefe.* ed. Helmut Sembdner. 2 vols. München, 1964.
*H. v. Kleists Lebensspuren.* Dokumente und Berichte der Zeitgenossen. ed. Helmut Sembdner. Bremen, 1957.
Baumgärtel, Gerhard. "Zur Frage der Wandlung in Kleists 'Prinz Friedrich von Homburg'," *Germanisch-Romanische Monatschrift,* XVI (1966), 264–77.
Benson, J. M. "Kleist's *Prince Friedrich von Homburg,*" *Modern Languages,* XLVI (1965), 98–103.
Blöcker, Günter. *Heinrich von Kleist oder das absolute Ich.* Berlin, 1962.
Böckmann, Paul. "Kleists Aufsatz über das Marionettentheater," *Euphorion,* XXVIII (1927), 218–53.
Ellis, John M. *Kleist's 'Prinz Friedrich von Homburg'. A Critical Study.* University of California Publications in Modern Philology, XCVII, Berkeley, 1970.
Fricke, Gerhard. *Gefühl und Schicksal bei Heinrich von Kleist.* Berlin, 1929.
–   "Kleists 'Prinz von Homburg'," in *Studien und Interpretationen.* Frankfurt, 1956, 239–63.
Gausewitz, Walter. "Kleist und der Kulturidealismus der Klassik," *Monatshefte,* LIII, 5 (October, 1961), 239–54.
Gearey, John. "Character and Idea in 'Prinz Friedrich von Homburg'," *Germanic Review,* XLII (1967), 276–92.
Gundolf, Friedrich. *Heinrich von Kleist.* Berlin, 1924.
Hafner, Franz. *Heinrich von Kleists "Prinz Friedrich von Homburg,"* Diss., Zürich, 1952.
Henkel, Arthur. "Traum und Gesetz in Kleists 'Prinz von Homburg'," *Neue Rundschau,* LXXIII (1962), 438–64.
Koch, Friedrich. *Heinrich von Kleist. Bewusstsein und Wirklichkeit.* Stuttgart, 1958.
Kohrs, Ingrid. *Das Wesen des Tragischen im Drama Heinrich von Kleists.* Marburg, 1951.
Kommerell, Max. "Die Sprache und das Unaussprechliche," in *Geist und Buchstabe der Dichtung.* Frankfurt a.M., 1962.
Korff, H. A. "Das Dichtertum Heinrich von Kleists," *Zeitschrift für Deutschkunde* (1933), 428–41.
Mathieu, Gustave. "The Struggle for a Man's Mind: A Modern View of Kleist's 'Prinz von Homburg'," *German Life and Letters,* XIII (1959/60), 169–77.

Müller-Seidel, Walter. "Heinrich von Kleist und die Wahrheit des Menschen," *Stoffe, Formen, Strukturen,* eds. Albert Fuchs and Helmut Motekat. München, 1962, 331–44.
– "Kleists 'Prinz Friedrich von Homburg'," in *Das deutsche Drama I,* ed. Benno von Wiese. Düsseldorf, 1958, 385–404.
– *Versehen und Erkennen.* Eine Studie über Heinrich von Kleist. Köln, 1961.
Nehring, Wolfgang. "Kleists 'Prinz von Homburg' – Die Marionette auf dem Weg zum Gott," *The German Quarterly,* XLIV (March, 1971), 172–84.
Pascal, Roy. "'Ein Traum, was sonst?' Zur Interpretation des 'Prinz Friedrich von Homburg'," in *Formenwandel.* Hamburg, 1964, 351–62.
Samuel, Richard (ed.). *Prinz Friedrich von Homburg.* Berlin: Erich Schmidt, 1964.
Schlagdenhauffen, Alfred. *L'univers existentiel de Kleist dans le Prince de Homburg.* Paris, 1953.
Schwarz, Egon, "Die Wandlungen Friedrichs von Homburg," in *Festschrift für Bernhard Blume.* Göttingen, 1967, 103–25.
Silz, Walter. "On the Interpretation of Kleist's 'Prinz Friedrich von Homburg'," *Journal of English and Germanic Philology,* XXXV (1936), 500–16.
Thalheim, Hans-Günther. "Kleists 'Prinz Friedrich von Homburg'," *Weimarer Beiträge,* XI (1965), 483–550.
Weigand, H. J. "Das Motiv des Vertrauens im Drama Heinrichs von Kleist," *Monatshefte,* XXX (May, 1938), 233–45.


*Joint Authors*


Backhaus, Elisabeth E. *Schiller und Kleist: Intrige und Marionette: Das Problem des jugendlichen Helden,* Diss., U. of Conn., 1966.
Blume, Bernhard. "Kleist und Goethe," in *Heinrich von Kleist. Aufsätze und Essays,* ed. Walter Müller-Seidel. Darmstadt, 1967, 130–85.
Crosby, Donald. *Schiller and Kleist: Influence and Creative Kinship,* Diss., Princeton, 1955.
Daffis, Hans. "Goethes 'Tasso' und Kleists 'Prinz von Homburg'" *Das deutsche Drama,* I (März, 1919), 78–84.
Leber, Elsbeth. *Das Bild des Menschen in Schillers und Kleists Dramen.* Bern, 1969.
Rasch, Wolfdietrich. "Tragik und Tragödie. Bemerkungen zur Gestaltung des Tragischen bei Kleist und Schiller," *Deutsche Vierteljahresschrift,* XXI (1943), 287–306.
Wiese, Benno von. *Die deutsche Tragödie von Lessing bis Hebbel.* Hamburg, 1961.

# STUDIENREIHE ZUR GERMANISTIK

*German Studies in America:*

Bd. 1     Nordmeyer, Rubaijat von Omar Chajjam. 2. Aufl. 104 S., brosch. und Lwd., 1969.

Bd. 2     Richards, The German Bestseller in the 20th Century. A complete Bibliography and Analysis. 276 S., Lwd., 1968.

Bd. 3     Germer, The German Novel of Education 1792–1805. A complete Bibliography.and Analysis. 280 S., Lwd., 1968.

Bd. 4     Gerlitzki, Die Bedeutung der Minne in "Moriz von Craûn". 132 S., Lwd., 1970.

Bd. 5     Bowman, Life into Autobiography. A Study of Goethe's "Dichtung und Wahrheit". 162 S., Lwd., 1971.

Bd. 6     Putzel, Letters to Immanuel Bekker from Henriette Herz, S. Pobeheim and Anna Horkel. 108 S., Lwd., 1972.

Bd. 7     Geldrich, Heine und der spanisch-amerikanische Modernismo. 304 S., Lwd., 1971.

Bd. 8     Friesen, The German Panoramic Novel in the 19th Century. 232 S., Lwd., 1972.

Bd. 9     Novak, Wilhelm von Humboldt as a Literary Critic. 142 S., Lwd., 1972.

Bd. 10    Shelton, The Young Hölderlin. 282 S., Lwd., 1973.

Bd. 11    Milstein, Eight Eighteenth Century Reading Societies. A Sociological Contribution to the History of German Literature. 311 S., Lwd., 1972.

Bd. 12    Schatzberg, Scientific Themes in the Popular Literature and the Poetry of the German Enlightenment, 1720–1760. 349 S., Lwd., 1973.

Bd. 13    Dimler, Friedrich Spee's "Trutznachtigall". 158 S., Lwd., 1973.

Bd. 14    McCort, Perspectives on Music in German Fiction. The Music-Fiction of Wilhelm Heinrich Riehl. 154 S., Lwd., 1974.

Bd. 15    Motsch, Die poetische Epistel. Ein Beitrag zur Geschichte der deutschen Literatur und Literaturkritik des achtzehnten Jahrhunderts. 217 S., Lwd., 1974.

Bd. 16    Zipser, Edward Bulwer-Lytton and Germany. 232 S., Lwd., 1974.

Bd. 17    Rutledge John, The Dialogue of the Dead in Eighteenth-Century Germany. 185 S., Lwd., 1974.

Bd. 18    Rutledge Joyce S., Johann Adolph Schlegel. 321 S., Lwd., 1974.

Bd. 19    Gutzkow, Wally the Skeptic. Novel. A translation from the German with an Introduction and Notes by Ruth-Ellen Boetcher Joeres. 130 S., Lwd., 1974.

Bd. 20    Keck, Renaissance and Romanticism: Tieck's Conception of Cultural Decline as Portrayed in his "Vittoria Accorombona". ca. 128 S., Lwd., 1976.

Bd. 21    Scholl, The Bildungsdrama of the Age of Goethe. ca. 90 S., Lwd., 1976.

Bd. 22    Bartel, German Literary History 1777–1835. In Vorbereitung.

Bd. 23    Littell, Jeremias Gotthelfs "Käserei in der Vehfreud". In Vorbereitung.